4/14

DATE DUE

OC 24 '97		
DE 19 '97		
AP 27 '98		
MY 3 '00		
MY 31 '05		

DEMCO 38-296

T H E
MATURE
MARKET

A GOLD MINE OF IDEAS FOR TAPPING THE

50+

MARKET

Robert S. Menchin

PROBUS PUBLISHING COMPANY
Chicago, Illinois

This publication is designed to provide accurate and authoritative information in regard to the subject matter covered. It is sold with the understanding that the publisher is not engaged in rendering legal, accounting or other professional service.

Library of Congress Cataloging in Publication Data Available

ISBN 1-55738-236-0

Printed in the United States of America

KP

1 2 3 4 5 6 7 8 9 0

For Marilyn, Johnathan, and Scott

CONTENTS

CHARTS

TABLES

PREFACE

This book is addressed to the professional marketers who move the merchandise from the factories to the stores and ultimately to the consumer. It also speaks to the service marketers struggling for a larger share of the market in a highly competitive service-oriented society.

In addition to alerting industry to the opportunities inherent in an aging America, the purpose of this book is to help marketers understand a paradox—the validity of the mature market as a separate and distinct group of Americans with similar consumer needs and desires and the contradictory fact that it is not a homogeneous group. There are, in fact, more differences within the fifty-and-over segment of the population than there are between these mature adults and the other segments of our society.

How does one generalize about 62 million Americans whose only common denominator is that they were born before 1939?

Aside from that, the mature market is not an easy one to understand because it is constantly evolving and changing—today's generation of seniors bears little resemblance to the one that came before and the one will come after it. The forces that shaped this generation of older American are among the most volatile and dynamic in history and to a large extent their consumer behavior is a product of these experiences.

As a member of the group under study, I find that examining my own feelings and changing attitudes as a consumer is a useful check against the conventional wisdom of the experts. It is not unlike the medical researcher who uses his own body to test a new drug. An overly dramatic example, perhaps, but in marketing as in so many other things in life, the insights that come from personal experience are infinitely more dependable than those that come from distant observation. Growing old, which is what we are all doing all the time, is nevertheless, a highly personal and emotion-charged experience. There are certain aspects of aging that you can only know about by being there yourself.

The health care industry and other industries that have traditionally provided seniors with age-related products and services, have already targeted older adults, their heaviest users and best customers. Consequently, while health care products and services are included in the book, it is not covered in proportion to its importance in the mature market. By design, greater emphasis has been placed on industries which do not as yet have the older generation firmly in their sights. I want to talk to these industries about marketing the less obviously age-related products and services, those not typically associated with the older consumer—travel, food and beverages and retail establishments, for example. In trying to cover the full gamut of business opportunities in the mature market, I tried to emphasize those product and service areas that have not reached their full potential in this market.

Developments in the mature market suggest that industry is starting to look up and take notice. I would advise marketers interested in participation in this dynamic market to listen carefully to what older adults are saying about their needs and desires—you'll learn things about the mature market that will help you correct any misconceptions you may have. You'll learn things they don't teach in Marketing 101.

A book of this kind naturally draws data from a variety of sources. Information and statistics released by the U.S. government, particularly data generated by the Census

Bureau and the Department of Labor and the Senate Special Committee on Aging, have proven invaluable in providing a statistical overview of the older segment of the population. Magazine and newspaper articles on the subject have created leads to the people and organizations on the cutting edge of the mature market.

Voluminous studies by industry groups, media, universities, companies, marketing firms and research organizations have been a mixed blessing. Useful, because in a field where so little has been examined, every bit of new evidence is one small step toward knowledge; frustrating, because each of these studies uses different criteria and time frames, making comparison and the search for common ground difficult, if not impossible. If, as a result, I am often forced to compare apples and oranges, at least the fruit is counted.

Studies by some of the major research companies help in specialized areas of consumer behavior. Some studies, conducted for specific companies or industry groups are shaped to promote a particular point of view or validate a presumption. When a client has a vested interest in the outcome of a study, a pinch or two of skepticism will balance the scale. Then too, there are the many studies which might have proved useful but were, and still are, the proprietary research of the companies that own them. These studies are conducted at some expense to the sponsors and while we regret not being able to share this intelligence with the marketing community, they are entitled to the competitive advantage they gain by keeping their results close to the vest. If, in the end, the study is translated into marketing action, the general tenor of the study will be known to all.

Robert S. Menchin
Chicago, Illinois

ACKNOWLEDGEMENTS

Sammy Cahn, the song writer, was asked how he starts writing a song–"Does it start with the words or the music?" He replied, "It starts with a phone call."

This book too started with a phone call. My friend, Lee Rosler, the publisher of my previous book, "Where There's A Will" called from New York to say that he thought there was a market for a newsletter with financial investment advice for mature men and women. I gave it a good try but the newsletter, "After 60 Money Matters," never got off the ground. As is usually the case, one thing leads to another and I soon realized that the real subject here was the awesome numbers and spending power of older Americans and the marketing implications of these facts.

Probus Publishing agreed with me and then the work began. Many people helped. Here are some of them . . .

Don Fowles, at the Health and Human Services Administration on Aging.

Lee M. Cassidy and Nona Wegner at the Mature Market Institute.

Robert Forbes, Director, National Association of Retired Persons.

Allen Rohr, Vice President of Goldring & Company.

Leonard Hansen, CEO, Senior Publishers Group.

David Wolfe, of Wolfe Resources.
Charles Longino, Jr., Director of the Center for Social Research in Aging at the University of Miami.
Elaine Sherman, Professor of Marketing, Hofstra University.
Margaret Wilde, Director, Advanced Living Systems Division of the Institute for Technology Development.
Leo Rotelli, President, Rotelli Design Studio.

. . . and a special note of thanks to the skilled librarians at the American Marketing Association and the National Association of Retired Persons.

"*I answered a telephone survey the other day. This woman asked if I'd take a few minutes to answer some questions about the kind of movies I liked. I said, 'Sure.' She asked how many times a month I go out to the movies. I said, 'Three or four.' She said, 'Oh, good.' Then she wanted to know about my work and my income. All good. Then she asked how old I was. I said, 'Fifty.' She said, 'Thank you,' and hung up.*"

OVERVIEW

"Will you still need me,
will you still feed me,
when I'm 64?"

The Beatles

ANTICIPATING THE SILVER DECADE

When a psychologist asked the notorious Willie Sutton why he robbed banks, he answered, "That's where the money is."

For the thousands of businesses across the nation catering to America's aging population, that reasoning is just as sound.

As the mature market emerges from relative obscurity and becomes larger and more visible, more and more opportunity-seeking companies will focus their marketing efforts on the millions of American men and women who have reached and lived beyond the half-century mark. By almost any measure—numbers, purchasing power, needs and desires, spending patterns and accessibility—the senior population of the United States represents a vast market for goods and services. From Freedent chewing gum at 50 cents a pack (they won't stick to dentures) to Rolls Royce automobiles at $135,000 (a stylish way to get from here to there), the best prospects are the men and women born before 1938.

One out of every four people in the nation is over fifty years of age, a total of more than 62 million men and women. They have a combined annual income of more than $900 billion and more than $160 billion in discretionary income—more than double the per capita discretionary income of younger age groups.

As a group, today's seniors live longer, healthier and more financially secure lives than any previous generation of older Americans. They are better off and dramatically different than the older population just a generation ago. As a group, their attitudes, lifestyles and values are more dynamic, their mental abilities sharper and their physical condition stronger.

America's 50+ population is numerically and proportionately larger than at any time in history. This is one of the fundamental facts shaping our economy, and is destined to become a dominant factor in consumer marketing. Now and well into the 1990s, there is both challenge and opportunity for American enterprise seeking profits by serving the insatiable demands of the nation's aging population.

The aging of America will have a profound effect on our society as both the government and private sector strive to keep pace with the needs of this exploding population. Already one-quarter of the total population, the number of mature Americans will grow even larger and become the dominant consumer group in the nation as the first of the

Number of Americans in Various Age Segments
Total U.S. population, 1987: 243.9 million. Percent of Total

	How Many	Percent of Total Population
50 and over	62.7 million	25.7 percent
55 and over	51.8	21.3
65 and over	29.8	12.2
70 and over	19.9	8.2
80 and over	6.3	2.6
50 to 54	10.9 million	4.5 percent
55 to 64	22.0	9.0
65 to 69	9.8	4.1
70 to 74	7.7	3.2
75 to 79	5.7	2.4

Source: U.S. Bureau of the Census, Current Population Reports, Series P-25, No. 1022.

nation's 76 million baby boomers turn 50 in the middle of this decade.

Catering to the needs and desires of this burgeoning mature market will be the growth industry of the 1990s.

A Century of Progress

A confluence of many factors contribute to the relatively-good general health and financial security of today's mature Americans.

Major medical advances and better nutrition and preventative health measures have added quality years to many lives. Consequently, new attitudes and changing perceptions of aging emerged and contributed to more active and involved lifestyles. Of course, these longer, more vibrant lives did not arrive without a price tag.

Fortunately for many older Americans, four decades of general prosperity enabled them to accumulate sizable nest eggs. In addition, Social Security, expanded corporate pensions, and for many, appreciation in the value of their mortgage-paid up home helped contribute to their financial well-being.

In the 1990s, many of the health and financial developments that have been evolving throughout the 20th century—which make possible the active lifestyles and relatively high standard of living that our older population enjoys, will come to even greater fruition.

Although many firms have become rich and successful catering to the mature market, it is a market that is for the most part, untapped. Visible marketing efforts directed at older consumers have been the exceptions rather than the rule; outmoded and false perceptions about the nature and potential of older consumers kept many companies from full participation in the mature market. It will not remain untapped for long. It is too large and too powerful a force at the checkout counter to be ignored.

In Search of Nomenclature

Journalists, legislators and marketers are searching for a label that describes the older men and women in our population. The debate about nomenclature is symptomatic of a new identity: the old labels just don't fit anymore.

"Old people," carries a stigma, "Senior citizens," mocks many who are old but denied the respect of seniority and doesn't account for the fact that they may or may not be citizens. "Retiree," won't do since many older Americans are at work and some, homemakers, for example, never held a salaried job from which to retire. "Elderly," is not an

50 and Over, a Growing Force

Line shows projection to the year 2020 of the number of people in the U.S. 50 years old and older, starting with an estimate for July, 1986, in millions. Bars show the percent of the population 50 and older.

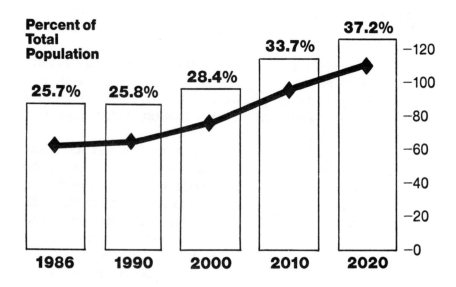

Source: Census Bureau.

accurate description of many people who are active and energetic despite the number of candles on their birthday cake.

A contest was held in Japan to find the best term for the later stages in life. As reported in "Ageing International"—yes, that's how they spell it—the previous term, *rojin* ("elderly") was considered inappropriate for today's active older citizen in Japan. The winning label: *jitsunem*, or, the "age of fruition."

Not to be outdone, *Modern Maturity* magazine came up with its suggestion for the American equivilant: "Emeritan," which combines merit, ermerit (to deserve), emerited (skilled through experience), emeritus (one who has served his time) and the word "American." Logical, but perhaps too formal to catch on. Nor is the designation of the travel newsletter for seniors that calls its readers "chronologically gifted" likely to enter the language, but it does strike a positive note.

No. Until the wordsmiths come up with a better alternative, we will stick to the mundane but generally understood, "senior," "mature" and "older American." While these terms will be used generically and interchangeably, the reader will find that the data and studies cited throughout have terminologies and/or definitions of their own. Whenever possible, the terms and labels that are integral to a study have been preserved, but defined for the reader, usually by age group: i.e., "age 50 to 65" or "65 and over." Unless otherwise noted, the terms used throughout are meant to describe, in general, the vast population that is 50 years and older.

References to "us" ("we" and "ours," etc.,) refer to a collective "us" and are used to represent society—and not just that portion of society of a certain age, but *all* of society. How we look at older people should include how others see them, as well as how they see themselves. As evidenced throughout this book, a stark "us and them" approach leads to an alienation of seniors in the marketplace, while a more empathetic one is rewarded. In order to cultivate this attitude of empathy, readers of all ages may, perhaps, keep in mind that this is one market of which we will all one day (hopefully!) be a part.

Finally, in searching for acceptable definitions of age segmentation (and Chapter One explores this in detail), it is important to note that today's mature market is still evolving and, in essence, defining itself. More importantly here, it is defining itself, literally and figuratively, through what it will and will not "buy into."

PART ONE
THE MARKET

"To me, old age is always fifteen years older than I am."

Bernard Baruch

THE OLDER MARKET: GROUPS AND SUBGROUPS

Multitudes

The number of people over the age of 50, is greater than the population of Great Britain, France or Italy. At the turn of the century, this population will grow by 20 percent, from over 62 million, to over 75 million.

Currently, about 30 million (one of every eight) people are over age 65, a number greater than the population of Canada or Argentina. The number of Americans age 65 and over increased by 2.8 million, or 11 percent, since 1980, compared to an increase of four percent for the under 65 population. *In fact is, one-quarter of all Americans who have ever lived to age 65 are alive today.*

People are living longer; a baby born in 1900 could expect to live 47.4 years, while a baby born in 1985 could expect to live 74.7 years. In the early part of this century, increases in life expectancy were due to fewer infant deaths, but most of the increased life expectancy since 1970 is the result of longer life among the middle-aged and elderly population.

Americans who reached their 65th birthdays in 1985 could expect, on average, to live another 16.8 years. Since

1900, life expectancy at age 65 has advanced significantly. Older men gained 3.1 years from 1900 to 1985 and older women gained 6.4 years in the same period. Greater longevity prolongs the opportunity for accumulating experience and money, and allows for all kinds of change: in jobs, marriage partners, and in new roles in later life. Years are added to relationships with spouses, parents, relatives and friends whose lives are also extended.

Longer life only partially explains today's large numbers and proportion of older individuals. The primary cause is an increase in the annual number of births prior to 1920 and after World War II. The aging of those born before 1920, along with a dramatic decline in the birth rate after the mid-1960s, has contributed to the overall aging of America. If, as expected, the trend toward smaller families and childless marriages continues, the decline in the proportion of young people in our population will continue and the graying of America will accelerate.

According to a Conference Board study sponsored by CBS, in the next fifteen years, the nation's total adult

The Aging of America

The population of the U.S. has been growing at a steady pace over the past center. But no segment of the population has grown faster than the 65 and over bracket.

Year	Population over 65 in millions
1900	3.1
1920	4.9
1940	16.7
1980	25.7
1987	29.8
Projected	
2000	34.9
2010	39.2
2030	64.6
2050	67.4
2080	73.1

Source: U.S. Department of Commerce, Bureau of the Census.

population will grow by 14 percent, but the number of those over 50 will increase by about 23 percent. The rate of growth for those age 50 to 65 will increase slightly faster, but the 75 and over population will explode by close to 50 percent.

Numerically, most of the growth in the older population over the next fifteen years will be accounted for by the younger old. Persons over 50 will increase by slightly more than 14 million. Of that number, more than 8 million will be age 50-65, fewer than a million will be 65-75 and about 5.5 million will be 75 and over.

Speaking to the interests of enterprising business people with goods and services to sell, the Conference Board study points out that "the biggest increase will be among those who are still fully active economically." From a marketing standpoint, this trend amounts to nothing less than a mandate for the reevaluation of current strategies and practices.

For years, the great marketing thrust in the U.S. was focused on young adults. The rich, acquisitive, ready-to-try-new-things Yuppies were the darlings of Madison Avenue. Marketers of everything, from breakfast cereals to luxury cruises, focused their efforts on catering to young Americans. It is not difficult to understand—the youth orientation served them well for over two decades. The sheer size of the post-World War II youth market was reason enough to pay attention. Moreover, decision makers in corporate America, themselves a rather young group, found it easy to relate to consumers their own age with the same passion for foreign travel, new cuisines, imported clothes and sports cars. Consequently, they continued to court their young, upwardly-mobile prospects while neglecting the less conspicuous, but more stable, spending power of the Yuppies' fathers and mothers. For the most part, older Americans were perceived as penny-pinching senior citizens in rocking chairs—traditional, conservative and just-plain-dull in their shopping and spending behavior.

The profound changes in demographics and in the economy have brought about a significant shift in perceptions. Increasingly, older Americans are seen as active consumers and likely prospects for many goods and services—expensive running shoes, upscale restaurants and luxury automobiles to name just a few. These changes call for a shift in marketing focus, a shift that is likely to become prevalent and more pronounced in the years ahead. Baby boomers are older, the birth rate has declined and medical breakthroughs have raised life expectancy—all creating a rise in the nation's median age. In addition, financial pressures on the lifestyles of the younger generation created ripples in the marketplace.

A bulletin by the Howard/Marlboro Group, a research and marketing organization, helps us to understand why the Yuppies may not be the spending champions they once were: "Finally, their envied and awesome discretionary buyer power is being threatened by a jittery stock market, by high mortgage payments and, in many cases, by a cutback to a single paycheck as many Yuppie wives or husbands choose to stay home with the kids."

Thus, the outdated mindset of yesterday is giving way to the demographic realities of today. The marketing target now moves from the Yuppies to the people that brought them into the world, their mothers and fathers. (Besides, if the baby boomers reach their maturity in the middle of the next decade, can the Yuppies be far behind?)

Marketers are responding to these shifts in demography and focus by adding older men and women to their marketing teams—a concept that is gaining ground with corporate decision-makers. Here, we address the potentiality of the mature market in terms of its sheer magnitude and breadth. Later in this chapter, we examine ways to segment and define this vast population by subgroups that are meaningful from a marketing perspective. However, in seeking valid classifications and definitions for this market, one must first consider how older people perceive and define themselves.

Ten Major Trends

Catering to the needs and desires of America's older population will be the growth industry of the 1990's. These ten major trends will make that statement a reality:

1. The more than sixty million Americans 50 years of age and over represent a larger number of seniors than ever before in history.

2. The senior population represents an increasingly larger proportion of the total U.S. population.

3. As a group, today's seniors are healthier and more active than previous generations of older Americans.

4. With dramatic increases in life expectancy, the current older population will have many more years of life.

5. Today's seniors have a more positive self-image and a more active lifestyle.

6. Todat's seniors are more financially secure and have more disposable income than any other population segment.

7. The trend toward earlier retirement gives seniors more years of free time and leisure

8. There are many more women than men in the older segment of the population.

9. As the total U.S. population becomes older, society's attitude toward older men and women and personal perceptions of aging have become more positive.

10. Even greater growth in the number and changes in the character of the older generation lie ahead in the 1990s as the first of the huge Baby Boomer population becomes seniors.

Perceptions of Age

"What age would you be if you didn't know what age you were?"

This question by legendary baseball pitcher Satchel Paige makes a perceptive statement about aging: a great deal of it is in the mind of the beholder.

Teenagers, for example, see themselves as being older in order to do all the glamorous, interesting things that people in their twenties get to do. Older persons, on the other hand, perceive themselves as being five to ten years younger than their chronological age. Elaine Sherman, assistant professor of marketing at Hofstra University, says that the difference between chronological age and perceived age grows as a person grows older and "seniors often buy products that are in conjunction with their perceived age."

A study by *U.S. News and World Report*, based on data by Market Facts Inc., addressed another aspect of aging: the age that adults, at different times in their lives, consider others to be "old." Of the young adults who respond to the study, 21 percent said that they consider people at age 50 to 59 as old, and 27 percent said that they considered 60 to 69 as old.

In contrast, 33 percent of the respondents in the 45-54 age group considered ages 70-79 as old. More than one-third of those age 65 and over placed "old" at 80-89. Among the mature, old age starts five to ten years from their present age.

While chronological age is fixed by date of birth (and necessarily important for government records, insurance applications, eligibility for beneifts, etc.) it is not, in itself, a basis for marketing strategy. Marketers must examine the self perceptions of the mature consumer, and reevaluate their own ideas on aging accordingly.

One way to update our perceptions of todays older Americans is to consider their famous contemporaries. The popularity of certain role models can serve as a barometer for the self-perceptions and aspirations of an entire generation.

Many of our most visible government officials, both appointed and elected, are older Americans. When Ronald Reagan, at age 78, stepped down after eight years in office, 65-year-old George Bush took over the Presidency after a grueling election campaign. The average age of the Supreme Court Justices is 70. More than one-third of our state governors are over 55 and almost one-fourth of the 436 members of the House of Representatives are over 60, as are almost one-third of the U.S. Senators.

These men and women are not the exceptions, but rather typical of today's mature adult; in their own circles, many are as active and involved as the most important people of our time. They are participating in ways that they never could earlier in their lives, and, every day, they are

Life Expectancy at Birth and Age 65 by Sex and Calendar Year, 1900–2050

	Male		Female	
	At birth	*At age 65*	*At birth*	*At age 65*
1900	46.4	11.3	49.0	12.0
1910	50.1	11.4	53.6	12.1
1920	54.5	11.8	56.3	12.3
1930	58.0	11.8	61.3	12.9
1940	61.4	11.9	65.7	13.4
1950	65.6	12.8	71.1	15.1
1960	66.7	12.9	73.2	15.9
1970	67.1	13.1	74.9	17.1
1980	69.9	14.0	77.5	18.4
1990	71.4	14.5	78.9	19.2
2000	72.1	14.8	79.5	19.5
2010	72.4	15.0	79.8	19.8
2020	72.7	15.2	80.1	20.1
2030	73.0	15.4	80.4	20.3
2040	73.3	15.6	80.7	20.6
2050	73.6	15.8	81.0	20.8

Source: Social Security Administration; Social Security Area Population Projections, 1984; Actuarial Study No. 92, *Aging America, 1985–86 Edition.*

disproving the stereotype of a passive, uninvolved senior population.

Many people also think of age in relation to the entertainment stars with whom they grew up. Here then are the young stars (in their fifties) that are now part of our mature population: Robert Redford, Warren Beatty, Mary Tyler Moore, Burt Reynolds, Shirley McLaine, Sophia Loren, Michael Caine, Elizabeth Taylor, Clint Eastwood and Sean Connery.

If these famous "fifties" are still part of the young old, what about 60-plus Dick Clark and Audrey Hepburn? Also in their sixties, Paul Newman, Bea Arthur, and Charles Bronson. In their seventies: Robert Mitchum, Dinah Shore, Kirk Douglas, Gregory Peck and Gene Kelly. Many of these stars are still playing romantic roles in action-packed movies and TV shows. The message to marketers is clear— "old" just isn't what it used to be.

Shades of Gray

Older persons, like their younger counterparts, are not a homogeneous group. Helen Harris, of Helen Harris & Associates, a Connecticut marketing group, calls the mature market a "moving target" made up of a "rich mosaic of lifestyles."

In fact, the differences among older Americans is greater in every way than the differences within younger age groups. Once you have segmented the men and women 50 and over from the rest of the population, then the segmentation process begins in earnest. For effective marketing, dividing the mature market into meaningful categories *within* the broad 50 and over population segment is as important as separating the young and middle-aged from the older consumer.

In his book, *Market Segmentation* (Probus, 1987), consultant Art Weinstein reports that in a survey of over three hundred marketing executives, segmentation is ranked as the third-most-important marketing pressure point (of eighteen functional areas tested), but "few companies use this marketing tool to its full potential."

Just as there is diversity within the senior population, there are differences in the ways that marketing professionals and research organizations segment the mature market. Each chooses a segmentation approach that will yield data and provide insight pertinent to that segment of the older population that holds the greatest potential for a particular line of products or services. Despite substantial research, it is often difficult to find precise answers to the questions that marketers are asking about the mature market. Among other things, differences in age breakdowns, time frames and research approaches make comparative conclusions difficult. Even so, almost all of the existing segmentation analyses, individually and collectively, provide information about the world of the mature consumer. Equally important, they suggest some of the many different ways that marketers can design their own segmentation categories to yield practical data relevant to specific marketing problems.

Two large advertising agencies, J. Walter Thompson and NW Ayer, have devoted some effort to segmenting the mature market and each agency has come up with its own unique approach. J. Walter Thompson segments the market into four groups: *Active Affluents, Homemakers, Active Retireds* and *Disadvantaged and Other*.

According to the Thompson agency, the Active Affluents make up 40 percent of the older population. They are the largest and most sought-after segment of the mature market. Sixty percent of this group are married empty-nesters and roughly half of the couples in this group are double income households. This means plenty of disposable income, but a limited amount of free time. As a group, this segment of the population has a positive attitude about life, but a sense of anxiety about upcoming retirement.

Homemakers make up 22 percent of the market; 70 percent of this group are women and 25 percent are widowed. Many women in this category are adjusting to the home with a retired husband, and without children.

Active Retireds account for 15 percent of the older population; because they are leisure oriented, but don't want to be isolated. Housing developers consider them ideal candidates for senior housing. The Disadvantaged and Other make up 23 percent of the older population.

NW Ayer Advertising Agency of New York has its own way of dividing the senior population, an approach quite different from J. Walter Thompson's emphasis on lifestyle. Ayer segments the mature market into four categories, based on psychological and sociological forces: *Satisfied Selves* (38 percent of seniors); an open and secure group of individuals who think of themselves as exciting, sexy, successful and stylish dressers. *Worried Traditionalists* (31 percent); insecure, closed to new ideas, worried about crime. *Contented Traditionalists* (28 percent); secure but closed to new things, they don't feel sophisticated, energetic or happy and cling to the past. *60s In the 80s* (3 percent); open but insecure.

As the 50+ population becomes larger and more affluent, segmentation within the category becomes more urgent—and more difficult. Older persons have a wide range of lifestyles, activity levels and needs. To be successful, marketers have to be sensitive to the needs of various segments of the older population, and must be careful to avoid myths and stereotypes about aging.

The older segment is divided up into a series of diverse and overlapping submarkets defined by financial status, age, gender, location, health, work (employed vs. retired), education, marital status, size of household, housing and living arrangements. In all of these aspects, the senior population should be viewed not in terms of black-and-white but in various shades of gray.

Age Segmentation

At what age does one become a member of the mature market?

From an official government point of view, one becomes a senior citizen at age 65. The Social Security Administration uses 65 as the age at which it pays full benefits. The government takes its precedent from the forced retirement age created by Chancellor Otto von Bismarck in 1889 for Germany's social welfare system. The U.S. Census Bureau also defines old age as 65 and over, and since much of the demographic research is based on their statistics, this arbitrary "65" has become the popularly accepted threshold of old age, whether it continues to be valid or not.

In fact, most people in the United States today retire before 65. The majority begin to take their Social Security benefits at age 62 or 63. At ages 55 to 64 fewer than three of every four men are still in the labor force. At the same time, with continued good health and vigor, some men and women remain at work well into their 80s. Obviously, 65, or the age at which an individual retires, is no longer a clear border between middle age and old age.

Marketers, in designing sales strategies, generally consider 50 as the pivotal age at which consumers become part of the mature market. That's when important behavioral change occurs—diets change as people become more conscious of nutrition, changes occur in fashion preferences and in the ways in which individuals spend their time and money. Since our focus is on the older adult as a consumer, we will include everyone 50 and over within our scope of interest.

This pattern of needs in the life cycle of later years should not mislead the marketer into pigeonholing his prospective customer and assume that everyone within a certain age exhibits the same purchasing behavior. Very few people would make the mistake of stereotyping young or middle age people but, for some reason, there is a perception out there that all old people are alike. The opposite is true; older people are more different from each other than they were at earlier stages in life.

In an interview in *Psychology Today*, Bernice Neugareten, one of the nation's leading gerontologists, decries the stereotypes of age:

The American stereotype of the aged is based on the needy aged; it doesn't resemble the majority of old people, nor are old people a homogeneous group. The stereotype has it that as people age, they become more and more like one another. In truth, they become less and less alike.

If you look at people's lives, they're like the spreading of a fan. The longer people live, the greater the difference between them. A group of 18-year-olds is more alike than a group of 60-year-olds. To say a man is 60 years old tells you nothing about him except that he has lived for 60 years.

Creative marketing to the older population starts with recognition of the shared interests and common needs, as well as the differences and diversity of lifestyles, within the 50 and over age segment. Understanding the great range of interests and lifestyles within today's older population is the key to success in marketing to the mature. In many categories of goods and services, such as mainstream food and packaged goods, the need for a special marketing approach may not be necessary. There are, however, highly personal categories like fashion, clothing, personal care, health care and travel, where sensitivity to mature preferences, and possible physical limitations, are crucial to success.

For example, consultant Helen Harris segments the older market into four distinct age groups—50-64, 65-74, 74-84 and 85 and over. *Selling to Seniors* newsletter reported on Ms. Harris's comments on each of these age groups during the marketing sessions of an American Society of Aging conference. Ms. Harris found that:

- The 33 million seniors in the 50 to 64 category comprise a $573 billion market, that this age group is concerned with appearance, fitness and nutrition and that they are good prospects for exercise equipment, cosmetics, luxury cars, investment advice and travel. There are many new grandparents in this age group and they spend substantial sums on their grandchildren.

- The 17 million in the 65 to 74 age group make up a market worth $195 billion and that seniors in this group have the most free time. They are concerned about diet and choose lighter foods, use medicines that help them accomplish daily chores, and are good prospects for travel services, restaurants and leisure activities.

- The 9 million 75 to 84 year olds represent a $98 billion market. Their priority is health care and maintaining their independence; they spend 25% of their income on health services.

- Those over 85 comprise the fastest growing segment of the mature market. They need support services, including services in the home, and general health care.

There are literally dozens of ways that different organizations segment the mature market by age. The reader may find it useful to construct age segmentation categories that can relate to a particular line of products or services. A simple, but useful, way to segment by age is to group ages 50 to 64 as the "young old," group the 65 to 75 as "seniors" and categorize all those 75 and older as "elderly."

Gender

U.S. Census Bureau Statistics illustrate how the ratio of females to males varies dramatically with age. In the 30-to-34 year age group, for example, the number of men to women was evenly balanced at about 10 million each. For the 65 and over age group, however, there were 17 million women and 12 million men: older women outnumbered older men nearly three to two.

The disparity becomes even greater in the upper age ranges, by age 85 and over, there were only 40 men for every 100 women. Reflected in these figures is the fact that, on average, women live longer than men, consequently, women are more likely to end up living alone. Older women also average a longer period of retirement than older men.

Location

The geographic distribution of the senior population is another category in which preconceptions abound. Don't

The Mature Markets: 1985–1995
Though the "older" population (aged 55 to 64) will shrink slightly in the next decade, it will remain the largest segment of the mature market.

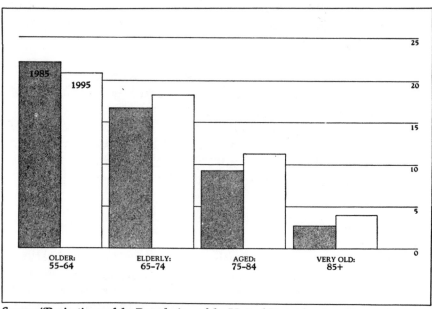

Source: "Projections of the Population of the United States by Age, Sex, and race: 1983–2080," Current Population reports, Series P-25, No. 952, Bureau of the Census, 1984.

90 percent of them live in Florida? Statistics on the geographic distribution of the senior population contain some surprises.

In 1985 about one-half of all persons 65 and older lived in eight states. California, New York and Florida had two million each; Illinois, Michigan, Ohio, Pennsylvania and Texas had over one million each.

Eleven states showed an increase of 17 percent or more in the number of seniors between 1980 and 1985: Alaska, Nevada, Hawaii, Arizona, New Mexico, South Carolina, Utah, Delaware, North Carolina, Washington and, yes . . . Florida.

Alaska, with the smallest senior population (18,000), experienced the largest percent increase: over 50 percent. It's a close call between the cities and the suburbs; about 32 percent of older people live in central cities while 39 percent live in the suburbs.

Florida has the largest proportion of residents 65 and over. However, according to a U.S. Senates Special Committee on Aging publication, *Aging America,* the proportion of elderly in Florida (17.7 percent) "is close to the proportion expected nationally in the year 2020." New York was the only metropolitan area in the nation with over one million older residents at the time of the last census.

Today's seniors tend to remain where they have spent most of their adult lives. In a study called "Geographical Mobility: March 1983 to March 1984" by Donald C. Dahmann of the Census Bureau, between 1983 and 1984, only 4.6 percent of older persons moved compared with 16.8 percent of persons of all ages.

With more younger people moving away, and large numbers of older people staying on, some areas of the country are aging at an accelerated rate. There are over 500 rural and small-town counties in which seniors 65 and over make up at least 15 percent of the total population. In 178 counties, seniors make up over 20 percent of the total. Many of these counties are in the nation's agricultural heartland. A large outward migration of the young and lower birth rates have created the high proportion of older persons in Iowa, Kansas, Missouri, Nebraska, South Dakota, Arkansas, Maine, Massachusetts, Rhode Island and Pennsylvania. Other areas with a high ratio of older people are places where seniors moved to in retirement such as—Florida, the Ozark plateau in Arkansas, and the Texas hill country.

The older population has grown in almost every region of the country. According to "The Graying of the Suburbs," an article by John R. Logan in *Aging Magazine,* the average suburban population in 1980 was 12 percent older Americans. In 1980, for the first time, a greater number of older persons lived in the suburbs (10 million) than in central cities (8 million) This large proportion of older persons resided in suburbs established before World War II.

Those seniors who move tend to move to warmer climates. The Sunbelt states are experiencing an aging of their population due to the influx of new residents in their early retirement years. Older people who move from one state to another are relatively affluent, well-educated individuals and usually move with their spouses. Disenchantment with metropolitan life and the lure of rural or small-town living motivate many such moves. Once the migration starts, it builds on itself as others move to be with family and friends who have already relocated.

There is a small, but significant, new trend called "countermigration" in which numbers of older people who moved to another state when they retired are moving back home. There are any number of reasons for this return to roots. Some simply miss their hometown, others are frail or disabled and require the care of friends and relatives, or they move back to enter homes for the aged. Findings from the Retirement Migration Project at the University of Miami's Center for Social Research in Aging show that Florida actually lost a substantial number of elderly migrants to states outside the Sunbelt such as Michigan, New York, Ohio and Pennsylvania—all states from which people migrate to Florida. For example, more than half of the 9,000 elderly Florida residents who moved to New York between 1975 and 1980 were born in New York. This was more than double the number who went back home to New York from Florida in the previous decade.

Health

The majority of younger old Americans are relatively healthy and are not as limited in activity as frequently assumed, even where there is some kind of chronic condition. Like other things in life, status depends a great deal on the self-assessment of the individual. Generally speaking, older persons have a positive view of their personal health. According to results of the 1986 Health Interview Survey conducted by the National Center for Health Statistics, 70 percent of older persons living in the community describe their health as excellent, very good, or good compared with others their age; only 30 percent report that their health is fair or poor.

It should be noted that this survey excludes the institutionalized 65plus population. Consequently, the healthy members of the older population are overrepresented. Nevertheless, the survey is a general measure of the overall health status of older persons in our society.

Work Status

With the passage of Social Security legislation in 1935, 65 became the magic number for when work ended and leisure began. In recent years, however, this concept of the "normal" retirement age has lost its validity. A 1978 Harris poll of American attitudes toward pensions and retirement found that almost two-thirds of retirees has left work before age 65. The median age of retirement in this sample was 60.6. Retirement, of course, is not necessarily the same as lack of employment. When the poll was taken, 81 percent of the retired respondents were not employed, but eight percent were employed part-time and five percent were working full-time.

Early retirement may be a permanent aspect of the working life in America. Even if there is an increase in the age of eligibility for full Social Security benefits, and mandatory retirement at 70 is eliminated, it probably will not have a major impact on future retirement age. Economic analyses by the National Commission for Employment Policy has shown that changing the age of eligibility for full Social Security benefits from age 65 to 67 would have a minimal effect on the actual age of retirement. People retire at a given age for a variety of reasons, such as health, private pension benefits, social expectations and long-held plans. Availability of Social Security is just one of the reasons for retirement, and not necessarily the major reason.

In 1986, 89 percent of the men and 62 percent of the women in the 50–54 age group were in the labor force. By age 60 to 64, only 55 percent of the men and 33 percent of women were working. Only 10 percent of the men and four

The 65+ Population by State 1986

State	Number (000's) 1986	Percent of all Ages 1986	Percent Increase 1980–86
U.S., total	29,173	12.1	14.2
Alabama	496	12.2	12.8
Alaska	18	3.4	55.3
Arizona	409	12.3	33.2
Arkansas	344	14.5	10.0
California	2,848	10.6	18.0
Colorado	294	9.0	18.9
Connecticut	423	13.3	15.8
Delaware	72	11.4	22.3
Dstr. of Columbia	77	12.2	3.1
Florida	2,071	17.7	22.7
Georgia	608	10.0	17.7
Hawaii	103	9.7	35.8
Idaho	112	11.2	19.7
Illinois	1,386	12.0	9.8
Indiana	657	11.9	12.1
Iowa	414	14.5	6.9
Kansas	330	13.4	7.7
Kentucky	449	12.0	9.5
Louisiana	454	10.1	12.3
Maine	156	13.3	10.8
Maryland	473	10.6	19.6
Massachusetts	794	13.6	9.2
Michigan	1,039	11.4	13.9
Minnesota	526	12.5	9.7
Mississippi	314	12.0	8.7
Missouri	694	13.7	7.0
Montana	99	12.1	17.3
Nebraska	217	13.6	5.7
Nevada	99	10.3	51.3
New Hampshire	119	11.6	15.2
New Jersey	981	12.9	14.1
New Mexico	144	9.8	24.5
New York	2,283	12.8	5.7
North Carolina	731	11.5	21.1

(Continued) State	Number (000's) 1986	Percent of all Ages 1986	Percent Increase 1980–86
U.S., total	29,173	12.1	14.2
North Dakota	88	13.0	9.6
Ohio	1,320	12.3	12.9
Oklahoma	411	12.4	9.3
Oregon	362	13.4	19.3
Pennsylvania	1,736	14.6	13.4
Rhode Island	142	14.6	11.8
South Carolina	355	10.5	23.6
South Dakota	99	13.9	8.4
Tennessee	590	12.3	13.9
Texas	1,583	9.5	15.5
Utah	133	8.0	22.2
Vermont	64	11.9	10.6
Virginia	606	10.5	19.9
Washington	520	11.7	20.5
West Virginia	261	13.6	9.8
Wisconsin	624	13.0	10.7
Wyoming	43	8.4	14.5

Source: Based on data from U.S. Bureau of the Census.

percent of the women age 70 and over were in the labor force.

The findings of a study by the RAI Division of Hearst Business Communications refute the generally held opinion that older individuals want to work. More than 70 percent of the retirees surveyed in the "Retired in America" study said that they were not interested in working at all. Retirees in this study were drawing a private pension and probably Social Security benefits. Consequently, 60 percent considered their annual income adequate and 94 percent reported that they did not receive any financial help from relatives.

Participation of older workers in the labor force has dropped significantly in the last three decades. In 1950, almost half of all men 65 and over were working. By 1986, only 16 percent of this group were working. In 1950, 10 percent of women 65 and over were working. By 1986, the figure dropped to 7 percent. Early retirement and a drop in self-employment explain the decline in the percent of older men and women at work.

Workers 55 to 64 comprise 10 percent of the total United States labor force; those 65 and over make up only 2.6 percent. In 1986, there were about 12 million workers age 55 to 64 and three million were 65 and over.

In recent years, the composition of our work force shows less agricultural and blue-color jobs and more white-collar and service positions. The Senate Committee on Aging contends that, "this shift from physically demanding or hazardous jobs to those in which skills or knowledge are the important requirements may increase the potential for older workers to remain in the labor force longer."

Education

The impact of education on consumer activity is significant for several reasons. Higher education means higher income and, consequently, greater purchasing power. An educated consumer is more receptive to a logical advertising approach and better quality merchandise and service. And finally, educated consumers buy more newspapers and books, take more trips abroad, and are better prospects for high-tech merchandise like VCRs and personal computers.

Using education to identify the best prospects within the older population is a practice that is advocated by TBWA Advertising. While it is skeptical of the willingness of older men and women to purchase expensive new products, the agency recommends that marketers of these products advertise primarily to the segment of the older market that is college educated, because these consumers are much more active in sailing, golf, tennis, photography, home entertaining and theater and concert attendance than older people without a college background.

Occupation of Older Workers by Age

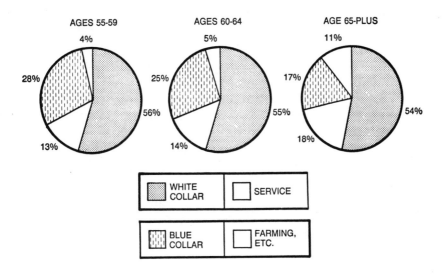

Note: White collar occupations include managerial/professional and technical/sales/administrative support.
Blue collar occupations include precision production/craft/repair, and operators fabricators/laborers.

Source: U.S. Department of Labor, Bureau of Labor Statistics. Unpublished data from the 1986 Current Population Survey.

According to William Bradford, TBWA's associate research director, "college-educated seniors are inclined to buy premium-priced, high-image brands, including many imported products." Bradford cites Dewar's scotch, Nikon cameras, Perrier water, Michelin tires and Grey Poupon mustard as favored brands among the more educated consumer.

The Wall Street Journal says that some ad agencies believe that concentration on education is myopic. The newspaper quoted Frankie Cadwell, president of Cadwell Davis Partners, an ad agency that is recommending to Reebok International that it advertise its walking and running shoes to the entire senior market. "The desire to be active and healthy cuts across the market," Caldwell said. "Older people today, no matter what their education, aren't just lying in hammocks and going fishing."

For a while, the younger generation had a substantial advantage over older people in the degree and quality of their education. However, the education gap between older and younger persons in the U.S. has narrowed over the last three decades and is expected to decrease further in the 1990s.

Between 1970 and 1986, the median level of education for persons 65 and over, based on school years completed, increased from 8.7 years to 11.8 years. By the end of the next decade, the median level of education for seniors is expected to be 12.4 years, an amount of education very close to the 12.8 for adults, age 25 and over.

The full impact of the strides made in the U.S. in fostering higher education and increased educational opportunities for all citizens, particularly women and minorities, will be felt in the next few years when people educated after World War II join the ranks of the older population.
Of course, formal schooling is not the only educational opportunity for seniors. Large numbers of older persons participate in adult education and part-time, noncredit courses. In the later years such education is pursued not only to advance careers, but often for personal enrichment. The U.S. Department of Education reports that in the year ending May 1984, 900,000 persons 65 or older, and 2.7 million 55 or older were enrolled in one or more adult education courses.

Marital Status and Living Arrangements

Marital status and living arrangements differ greatly between older men and older women. Most men spend their

Educational Attainment by Age

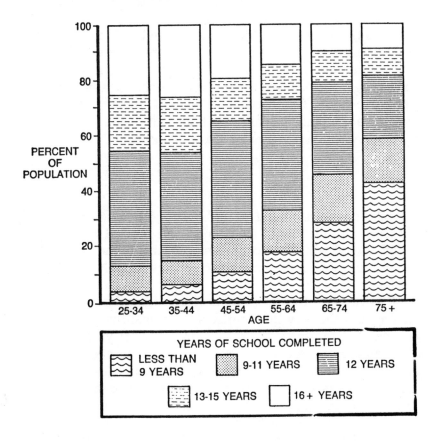

Source: U.S. Bureau of the Census. Unpublished data from the March 1986
Current Population Survey.

later years married in a family setting while most women
spend their later years outside of family settings.

Most older men remain married until they die, most
older women are widowed. Three factors create this situation: Men have a shorter average life expectancy so they
tend to predecease their wives. Men tend to marry women
who are younger than themselves. Men who are widowed
or divorced are more likely to remarry than are women in
these situations. The National Center for Health Statistics in

its "Advance Report on Final Marriage Statistics, 1984" found that older widowed men have remarriage rates over eight times higher than those of women.

Two-thirds of the older population who do not live in institutions live in a family environment. These statistics vary by gender, and the differences grow larger with advancing age. The Census Bureau reports that nearly four of every five men 75 and older lived with their spouses or other family members while less than half of the women in this age group lived in similar circumstances.

Housing

In 1987 there were almost 90 million households in the U.S. Of these, 19 million, or 21 percent, were headed by people age 65 and older. Older people represent a higher percentage of householders because their average household size is smaller.

It is difficult to make broad generalities about seniors' housing and the way that it affects their finances. For some, with paid up mortgages or modest mortgage payments, it is a valuable asset: the small monthly expenditures free up funds to allow for a higher standard of living. Also, equity in the home is an important part of the retirement nest egg. For others, burdened with high prevailing rents or newer mortgages with high monthly payments, housing costs can be a burden and dilute the funds available for spending on other things.

Marital Status of Older People, by Age, Sex
(excludes people in institutions)

Marital status	65+ Male	65+ Female	65–74 Male	65–74 Female	75+ Male	75+ Female
ALL RACES						
Total (thousands)	11,272	16,049	7,440	9,439	3,832	6,610
Percent	100.0	100.0	100.0	100.0	100.0	100.0
Never married	5.1	5.2	5.2	4.4	5.0	6.3
Married, spouse present	75.3	38.3	79.2	49.2	67.9	22.8
Married, spouse absent	1.9	1.7	1.9	2.1	1.9	1.1
Widowed	13.7	50.5	9.1	38.8	22.5	67.0
Divorced	4.0	4.4	4.6	5.5	2.7	2.7

Source: U.S. Bureau of the Census. Unpublished data from the March 1986 Current Population Survey.

Note: Percentage distributions may not add to 100.0 due to rounding.

Living Arrangements of Older People, by Age, Sex
(excludes people in institutions)

Living arrangement	65+ Male	65+ Female	65–74 Male	65–74 Female	75+ Male	75+ Female
ALL RACES						
Total (thousands)	11,272	16,049	7,440	9,439	3,832	6,610
Percent	100.0	100.0	100.0	100.0	100.0	100.0
Living with spouse	75.3	38.3	79.2	49.2	67.9	22.8
Living with other relatives	7.2	18.2	5.7	14.4	10.2	23.8
Living alone	14.9	41.3	12.7	34.6	19.2	51.0
Living with nonrelatives	2.5	2.1	2.4	1.9	2.7	2.4

Source: U.S. Bureau of the Census. Unpublished data from the March 1986 Current Population Survey.

Note: Percentage distributions may not add to 100.0 due to rounding.

Housing Costs as a Percentage of Household Income, By Age of Householder, Tenure, and Mortgage Status

	Age of householder				
		65+			
Tenure and mortgage status	Under 65	Total	65–69	70–74	75+
Owned, without mortgage	9.9	15.3	13.5	15.4	17.2
Owned, with mortgage	19.8	24.3	22.7	24.4	28.6
Rented	27.9	32.2	31.2	31.3	33.3

Source: U.S. Bureau of the Census. "Financial Characteristics of the Housing Inventory for the United States and Regions: 1983." Current Housing Reports Series H-150-83, Annual Housing Survey: 1983, Part C (December 1984) and unpublished data.

CHAPTER TWO

CONSUMER PROFILES AND PATTERNS

A Product of Their Times

Today's older Americans are the product of six decades of cataclysmic change. They have lived through wars, life-prolonging science and medical breakthroughs, the sexual revolution and the women's movement. Their early life was affected by the depression of the thirties, and, later, they participated in the post-World War II economic recovery: a period of expansion that is unprecedented in world history.

Although the relationship is not always obvious, these events influence mature consumer behavior in many ways. For example, World War II veterans received government benefits that gave them a head-start toward personal financial success—the GI Bill subsidized their education and low-interest VA-backup mortgages enabled them to purchase homes that subsequently appreciated in value. Many men and women currently enjoying a financially secure old age can trace their good fortune to the GI Bill and VA mortgages that became the foundation for their nest egg. In their later years, veterans qualified for low cost or free medical benefits and other privileges that lessen the economic concerns of old age.

It should be no suprise that no matter how much money they have now, people who lived through a devestating depression in their early formulative years are careful about money and concerned about getting value for each dollar. Many sociologists have observed a more hedonistic attitude in older persons and a willingness to spend more on self and personal indulgence. Many of today's seniors are less concerned with leaving inheritence for heirs and intend to enjoy their wealth and their money *now*.

Perhaps this is a result of older persons living long enough (with relative prosperity) to temper the caution of the earlier depression years. Or, living long enough to see their children become financially independent. Whatever the reasons, this attitude is best summed up by a popular bumper sticker that reads "I'm Spending My Grandchildren's Inheritence."

Thus the seeming contradiction: careful about money but willing to spend on self and enjoy life.

The sexual revolution that occurred during the lifetime of today's seniors has changed relationships and living arrangements for large segments of our population—the traditional family (husband at work, wife at home, a couple of kids), now accounts for less than one-fifth of American households. The older generation is also a part of the open lifestyle. While it is not always reflected in the statistics, many older men and women are living together, without the formalities of marriage, in order to maintain their financial independence and government benefits. In these cases, their consumer behavior would be similar to the married couple household.

Since women make up a disproportionately large part of the mature market, the consequences of the women's movement in America is being felt by those catering to today's older woman and will have even greater meaning to those planning to accommodate the large numbers of women who become part of the older generation with every passing day. Because of the women's movement, we have more older women working at higher salaries and with greater spending power. Moreover, women live longer and thus remain customers for a greater period of time; they spend more on beauty care, health products and clothing; they are the "natural shoppers," dear to the hearts of manufacturers and retailers alike.

Spending Power: Income Plus

With over 40 percent of the nation's discretionary income, the 55 to 74 age group is in the best financial shape of any age group ever. How did this happy state of affairs come about? How did the older generation, traditionally low man on the totem poll when it comes to sharing in the economic prosperity, rise to the top?

Aside from the post-World II gains, the first substantial gains in the income of older persons were made during the 1960s and early 1970s. These were due mostly to a general increase in the standard of living and improvements in Social Security and company pensions. The lengthened period of coverage for benefit credits and Social Security benefit increases between 1969 and 1972 brought real gains in seniors' income. Cost of living increases from 1968 to 1971 raised benefits by 43 percent, while prices increased by only 27 percent. In addition, the 1972 Social Security Amendments increased benefits another 20 percent.

Improvement in the economic status of seniors, as a result of these higher benefits, was dramatic. The poverty rate among those 65 and over was halved, declining from 28.5 percent in 1966 to 14.6 percent in 1974.

Economic stagnation in the late 1970s and early 1980s slowed real income increases for all age groups, but the impact was greater on the younger people still in the labor force than it was one the older segment. Real incomes of the younger group remained relatively constant during this period while real income of older persons rose—the result of growth in Social Security benefits for a new generation of retirees with better wage records. Automatic annual Social Security cost-of-living adjustments (COLAs), went into effect in 1975 and stabilized the real benefits of those already retired.

Since 1982, the median income of families with a head of-household age 65 and older rose in dollars from $18,309 in 1982 to $19,932 in 1986, an increase of nine percent. During this same period the poverty rate among those 65 and older has declined from 14.6 percent to 12.4 percent. Also, while the 1986 median income ($19,932) for older households was less than two-thirds (62 percent) of the median income of households age 25 to 64, the other benefits and resources available to older men and women greatly narrowed the gap.

Currently, the combination of income, assets and other economic advantages places them roughly on a par with younger adults in spending power. A study prepared by the U.S. Senate Special Committee on Aging* states that, "If all of these additional resources could be converted to a cash value, the economic status of the elderly as a group would becloser to that of the nonelderly."

Older Americans enjoy several economic advantages: favorable tax treatment of certain income, government in-kind transfers (Medicare, Medicaid, low rental housing, etc.), lifetime accumulations of wealth, and smaller family size. Adjusting for these differences, many economists agree that the financial status of the aged as a group is now such that they can, more or less, maintain in retirement the standard of living they enjoyed in their middle-age working years.

This conclusion is reinforced by the fact that the incidence of poverty among the aged is significantly less than that among the non aged. It is further supported by the Senate Committee's report on Aging in America. Referring to the non-cash resources of older persons, the report states that "some analysts contend that when these factors are taken into account, the average older person has economic resources roughly equivalent to those of younger persons."

Contrary to popular belief, the economic status of older Americans is far more varied than that of any other age

---

* The U.S. Senate's Special Committee on Aging has done extensive research on the older members of the nation's population. Unless otherwise noted, the Committee's publication, *Aging America, Trends and Projections, 1987-88 Edition* and U.S. Census Bureau data served as a source of the demographical data used here.

Income Sources of Units Aged 65 and Older

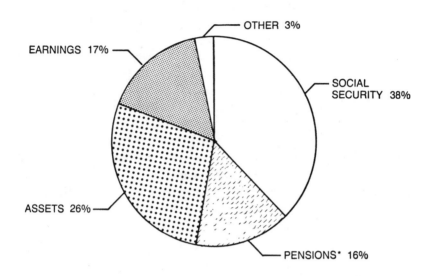

Note: Includes railroad retirement which accounts for about one percent
of income for age dunits. Railroad retirement has both pension and
social security components.

Source: Grad, Susan, Income of the Population 55 or over, 1986. Pub.
No. 13-11871, Washington: U.S. Social Security Administration,
forthcoming.

group. Some of our senior population are poor, others are
rich and some are quite wealthy. Most of the wealthiest
people in the nation are over 50.

A study by The Markle Foundation reports that 42 percent of Americans age 60 to 69 have income of $25,000 and
over. One in ten in this age group have incomes of $50,000
and over.

Assets

Interest and dividends on savings and investments and
rents from real estate, make up a substantial part of the in-

come of seniors. As a group, older Americans hold substantially more in assets than the younger segments of the population, a result of the normal life pattern in which people tend to accumulate savings, home equity and personal property over a lifetime.

The median net worth of households, headed by people age 65-and-over was $60,266 in 1984, compared to a median net worth for all households of $32,677. The age group with the largest median net worth ($73,664) was 55-64.

More than one-third of the wealth of the older generation exists in the equity in their homes. Nearly 75 percent of older persons own their homes—80 percent of those with mortgages paid up, "free and clear."

However, older people as a group have a smaller share of their equity in a business or profession, and a larger share than the younger segments of the population in liquid assets such as savings, checking, or money market accounts. In 1984, 30 percent of their net worth was in savings and checking accounts, compared to only 18 percent of the net worth of all households. Moreover, older people have a smaller share of their equity tied up in their homes than the younger people. In 1984, 39 percent of their net worth was equity in their home compared to 41 percent of the net worth of all households. However, more of the older Americans' homes are free of any mortgage.

According to the National Center for Home Equity Conversion, a non-profit organization in Madison, Wisconsin, there are 13.1 million homes, with a mean value of $62,400 per home, owned and lived in by older Americans. More than 80 percent of these are paid up and free of any mortgage. Substantial appreciation in the value of residential real estate in the past few decades has added to the assets of older Americans.

So many older Americans own their own mortgage-free homes, that they are often said to be "house-rich but cash poor." Reverse mortgage plans, which turn bricks into spendable dollars, have been developed to cope with this problem and they are gaining in popularity. They allow individuals to turn the value of their homes into cash, without having to move or repay the loan each month.

Home equity conversion (HEC) plans are relatively new in the United States, but they have been offered in European countries for some time. Still in the early stages of development, a variety of American HEC plans are available in certain parts of the country. As these plans spread to all segments of the older population, and gain in popularity, an enormous amount of heretofore locked-up cash will flow into the marketplace.

It is impossible to predict the actual amount of cash that will be freed because no one can estimate how many seniors will use Home Equity Conversion to supplement their income. However, a recent Congressional report indicated that older Americans have approximately $600 billion tied up in equity in their homes: an indication of the total spendable dollars that can potentially be unleashed for goods and services as these plans become more widespread. Figures issued by the Federal Home Loan Mortgage Corporation show a huge jump in home equity loans, which totaled $75 billion in 1985, up from only $2 billion in 1970.

Obviously, home equity loans and reverse mortgage plans hold the potential for a vast flow of cash to many older Americans and from them into the marketplace.

Discretionary Income

How much money is available for older Americans to spend after day-to-day needs are met?

Discretionary income, the money available to households after all basic, everyday expenditures have been made, is a crucial factor in measuring the potential of the mature market. Discretionary income statistics are somewhat arbitrary; that which some consider a luxury is an essential for others.

In a study by the Bureau of Census in collaboration with the Consumer Research Center of The Conference Board, households with spendable income at least 30 percent higher than the average of their group, were considered to have discretionary income.

Here are some highlights of that study . . .

- The age segment 40-65 has a substantially higher-than-average incidence of homes in the affluent earning brackets. Discretionary income is largely concentrated in that age group. They represent 40 percent of all homes, but account for well over half of all discretionary resources.

- Homes headed by persons 65 or older also represent an important segment of the luxury market because they are numerous and affluent. They represent 21 percent of the population, and 18 percent of all discretionary spending.

- While average discretionary income begins to decline for households headed by persons 60 and over, *per capita* discretionary incomes continue to increase at that age because household size is declining.

Over the years, the money available to consumers for luxury spending has been rising faster than total spendable income. Each year, as more of the affluent of our population enter their later years, millions of the middle class and a large number among the upper income brackets join the ranks of older households. This ongoing escalation is part of the dynamics of the rising prosperity of the nation's older generation.

The Affluent Elderly

There is a growing number of well-to-do, retired Americans and the degree of their affluence is growing as well. In an article in *American Demographics* entitled, "The Comfortably Retired and the Pension Elite," Charles Longing, Jr., director of the Center for Social Research in Aging at the University of Miami, provided some reasons for this phenomenon.

The World War II GIs who reaped the financial rewards of a 20-year economic expansion are now retiring. For their wartime service, they received a free college education from the GI Bill and a low-cost suburban-home loan from the FHA. During their careers, the GIs watched as a cost-of-living escalation clause was attached to their Social Security benefits. They also saw a federal law enacted that made their private pensions far more secure. Many of the former GIs also invested in stocks, rental properties, and securities as the economic boom began. The result today is an expanding number of upscale retirees.

In an introductory essay to a lengthy study on "The Economically Advantaged Retiree," Dr. Longing explains that so much research has been focused on the elderly poor and so little on the more affluent older Americans because

Distribution of Total Net Worth by Type of Asset in Different Age Categories

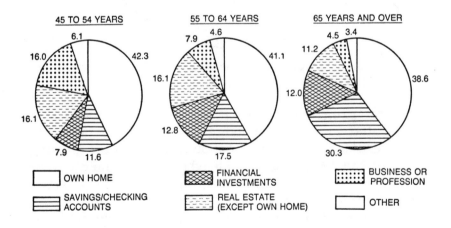

Source: U.S. Bureau of the Census. "Household Wealth and Asset Ownership: 1984." Current Population Reports Series P-70, No. 7 (July 1986).

Households with Discretionary Income by Age
Total Discretionary Income = 100%

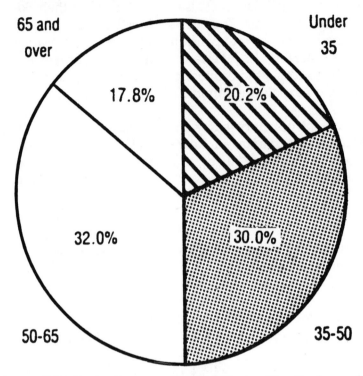

Source: Joint Study, Consumer Research Center, The Conference Board and the United States Bureau of the Census.

Federal programs that serve the poor required and generated greater knowledge of the elderly poor. He believes this has "drawn attention away from the growing part of the retired population who are economically advantaged. This relatively affluent subpopulation is served much more by the private sector than by the public sector. As it continues to grow and becomes a more influential part of the older population, therefore, it will generate vigorous market activity."

Dr. Longing believes that the emphasis on frailty and poverty has had the positive effect of increasing government benefits for older citizens, but "catering to negative stereotypes, however, may have increased the stigma of old age. The stigma burden affects the elderly, whether or not they are frail or poor."

How many retired people are affluent, and where do they live?

Using information extracted from the 1980 census and defining their segment as people 55 years of age or older who had not been in the labor force for one year, the Center for Social Research in Aging examined two groups of relatively affluent retired Americans: the "comfortably retired" and the "pension elite." The comfortably retired live in households with incomes more than twice the poverty level and includes most older Americans who have discretionary income. The pension elite are retired people who receive money from three sources, Social Security, pensions and assets.

According to the Center's findings, in general, the share of the retired who are "comfortable" is greatest among those aged 55 to 64 (59 percent) and drops in the older age groups. The pension elite have a different age distribution; they are clustered in the 65-to-74 age group, with 12 percent in this category. Nine percent of those age 75 and older and only 5 percent of those 55 to 64 are members of the pension elite.

Since the last Census was conducted in 1980, the Center's conclusions, based on that census, should be viewed merely as the foreshadow of a major demographic trend that gathered momentum at the end of the 1980s and will reach its full potential in the 1990s. In 1980, the 25 year old World War II GI was only 60 years old and too young for Social Security and many private pension benefits. A similar study based on the 1990 Census will reflect the period during which most GIs entered retirement age and, therefore, will show a dramatically larger number and proportion of both the comfortably retired and the pension elite.

The Center's findings on the geographic distribution of the upscale retired are less subject to updating and correction by the 1990 census, since they reflect already estab-

Retiring Comfortably

There are nearly 15 million people who are comfortably retired in the U.S. and another 3 million who are among the pension elite.

Total number of comfortably retired and pension elite by state, and as a percentage of all retired people aged 55 and older by age and state, 1980

	Comfortably Retired				Pension Elite			
	total	55-64	65-74	75+	total	55-64	65-74	75+
Total	14,771,320	59.1%	51.1%	37.5%	2,894,260	4.7%	12.3%	8.6%
Alabama	190,260	44.7	35.4	27.9	29,040	3.1	7.2	5.6
Alaska	8,860	65.4	59.3	45.6	860	3.0	10.5	3.4
Arizona	219,320	62.1	59.8	49.5	45,020	6.2	16.2	11.7
Arkansas	125,940	42.9	36.6	23.7	22,500	3.7	8.3	5.6
California	1,608,600	65.1	59.7	45.7	308,960	5.6	15.3	10.6
Colorado	150,580	66.2	55.8	40.2	27,760	5.0	14.0	9.3
Connecticut	238,100	70.9	62.7	47.5	53,040	6.1	18.5	12.4
Delaware	39,940	66.3	56.9	44.9	7,840	6.0	16.1	9.7
District of Columbia	44,340	53.3	55.3	49.9	7,460	3.2	12.3	10.0
Florida	1,140,300	63.0	61.0	49.1	239,520	7.1	15.7	11.6
Georgia	242,480	47.8	39.2	31.8	34,460	3.1	7.4	5.8
Hawaii	57,340	70.9	64.0	57.5	9,100	5.1	14.6	9.4
Idaho	48,100	59.3	48.9	32.5	7,020	3.2	10.5	5.4
Illinois	757,460	64.6	58.6	44.1	144,640	5.2	14.5	10.3
Indiana	338,320	63.9	54.1	38.4	73,000	5.7	15.4	10.7
Iowa	190,680	63.9	55.0	34.7	30,620	4.6	10.8	7.1
Kansas	147,980	63.9	53.9	35.1	23,700	3.5	11.0	7.4
Kentucky	190,920	45.1	39.9	31.4	33,020	4.0	9.1	6.5
Louisiana	190,740	48.4	38.5	30.9	24,020	2.7	6.7	5.1
Maine	67,200	52.4	45.5	31.9	14,740	4.8	12.9	8.7
Maryland	280,780	67.2	59.8	47.9	55,720	5.6	16.3	11.9
Massachusetts	408,780	63.9	54.6	39.7	82,380	4.8	14.3	9.7
Michigan	593,600	63.2	54.5	39.1	134,260	6.6	16.2	11.8
Minnesota	230,100	63.1	50.6	32.1	47,400	5.5	12.7	8.9
Mississippi	104,200	38.7	30.5	24.2	12,820	2.5	5.0	3.3

Total number of comfortably retired and pension elite by state, and as a percentage of all retired people aged 55 and older by age and state, 1980

	Comfortably Retired				Pension Elite			
	total	55-64	65-74	75+	total	55-64	65-74	75+
Missouri	325,640	56.2	48.7	34.0	63,200	4.5	12.2	8.2
Montana	42,140	59.6	47.5	30.3	7,080	5.7	9.6	6.8
Nebraska	93,200	63.4	51.7	32.8	12,560	3.4	8.2	6.1
Nevada	45,320	67.9	60.6	43.7	6,800	5.4	12.3	7.8
New Hampshire	56,580	64.8	51.8	38.9	13,300	8.1	15.3	10.6
New Jersey	581,080	68.3	61.6	49.4	116,080	5.3	16.5	11.8
New Mexico	65,920	53.7	48.1	35.7	11,180	3.9	11.4	7.7
New York	1,272,760	60.0	55.0	42.7	275,220	5.9	15.5	10.5
North Carolina	271,100	47.9	39.4	31.9	40,780	3.2	8.0	6.0
North Dakota	32,860	60.6	47.6	28.1	3,820	2.0	7.4	4.5
Ohio	738,120	63.4	55.3	40.9	158,200	5.8	16.2	10.6
Oklahoma	166,480	50.3	42.5	29.1	25,900	2.7	8.9	6.1
Oregon	181,420	62.9	56.5	38.7	42,180	6.4	16.3	11.9
Pennsylvania	984,820	62.8	55.4	42.3	224,940	6.2	16.8	11.9
Rhode Island	69,900	62.7	51.5	37.4	14,840	5.5	13.9	9.9
South Carolina	136,860	47.1	40.0	31.6	20,760	3.7	8.3	5.5
South Dakota	32,760	52.3	42.7	23.6	4,320	2.5	6.6	4.7
Tennessee	232,660	46.8	39.2	30.1	39,780	3.8	8.9	6.5
Texas	681,200	57.3	46.1	33.3	103,820	3.8	9.5	6.6
Utah	67,440	67.3	59.3	39.6	12,200	4.9	13.1	10.6
Vermont	30,900	57.8	50.3	38.2	7,660	6.3	15.5	12.1
Virginia	306,940	58.2	52.8	41.3	53,820	4.6	12.5	9.1
Washington	280,640	67.7	58.9	39.2	64,720	6.4	18.3	11.7
West Virginia	135,960	50.2	45.5	35.5	26,740	4.8	11.7	9.1
Wisconsin	304,620	65.2	54.4	35.9	72,980	6.8	16.3	10.7
Wyoming	19,080	62.7	52.4	34.9	2,480	1.8	9.3	7.3

Note: The comfortably retired live in households with incomes more than double the poverty level. The pension elite receive income from three sources: Social Security, pensions, and assets.

Source: Center for Social Research in Aging, University of Miami, Coral Gables, Florida.

lished patterns. According to the Center's analysis of the 1980 census, California has over 1.6 million of the comfortably retired, followed by New York and Florida with more than one million each. The same three states each have over 200,000 of the pension elite. This is to be expected, since these are three states with large numbers of older residents, but the proportions reveal an unexpected cluster of states with a large share of the comfortably retired.

Only 59 percent of Americans age 55 to 64 are comfortably retired, but the proportion of this group is greater than 66 percent in Connecticut, Hawaii, Maryland, Nevada, New Jersey and Washington. Just 51 percent of Americans age 65 to 74 are comfortably retired, but more than 60 percent who fit this description live in Connecticut, Florida, Hawaii, Nevada and New Jersey. Only 38 percent of retirees 75 and older are comfortably retired nationally, but at least half reached the comfort level in Hawaii, Arizona and the District of Columbia with Florida and New Jersey close behind.

What do these states have in common? According to Professor Longing, "Arizona, Florida, Nevada and New Jersey are resort and retirement states. Connecticut is home to a large number of retired New York City executives. Hawaii has a large Asian population, and older Asians are more likely to live with their extended families than other Americans. This gives them a big advantage in our economic measure, which is based on total household income." The list of states with the largest shares of retirees among the pension elite is similar to the list for comfortably retired, but with the addition of Pennsylvania, Oregon and Washington.

Not surprisingly, The University of Miami study finds a concentration of upscale retirees at the local level in cities such as Fort Lauderdale and Palm Beach in Florida, and San Diego and Palm Springs in California. Alabama, however, is a good example of the many states which rank below the national income average as a state but contain a sizable concentration of upscale retired people in some places; Alabama has a large concentration of affluent elderly on the east coast of Mobile Bay.

New Economic Vitality from Old Money

What steel is to Pennsylvania and what automobiles are to Michigan, retirees are to Arkansas. Retirees have been coming to Arkansas in droves and pouring millions of desperately needed dollars into the state's economy. With its 14.3 percent retirees, Arkansas has become the second largest state in percentage of retirees. Only Florida, with 17.6 percent retirees, has a greater percentage of retirees relative to the general population.

In a study of one location, a three-county area near Hot Springs, Arkansas, retirees were found to receive 65 percent of their income from out of state but spend 88 percent of their income within the community. It is estimated that large retirement communities generally produce one service job for every eight residents. Hot Spring Village has produced even better results: It's 4,400 residents created 75 new local businesses and more than 1,400 new jobs.

Retired individuals continue to generate approximately $50,000 each in state tax revenue over the balance of their lifetimes as Arkansas residents. Dr. Jim Ott of Henderson State University says that, "If retirees were an employer, they would be the second largest in Arkansas."

Throughout the country, one finds examples of retirees pumping new economic vitality into distressed areas. Communities, tired of losing the battle to bring new industries into town, are finding that retirees are an industry in themselves. In many ways, retirees are better residents than the smokestack plants they've been trying to attract. Retirees contribute to the tax base and require little or no additional spending for police or schools. They pump fresh money into local banks but they don't pollute the streams or send noxious fumes into the air.

Oconee County, South Carolina, hit hard by a steep decline in its textile industry, has been transformed from a depressed area into one of the state's fastest-growing commercial counties by an influx of upscale migrants settling in Keowee Key, a popular and growing retirement community. The average household income of Keowee Key residents is above $90,000, more than four times the income in

Households with Discretionary Income by Age

	Households		Average Income		Spendable Discretionary Income		
	Number (thousands)	Proportion to households	Before taxes	After taxes	Aggregate (billions)	Average	Per capita
Total	26,409	31.5	$46,764	$34,562	$277.9	$10,525	$3,713
Under 25 years	1,195	21.0	32,821	25,287	7.7	6,444	2,833
25 to 29 years	2,472	26.1	41,595	31,079	18.9	7,654	2,867
30 to 34 years	3,355	34.8	44,289	32,534	30.3	9,021	2,799
35 to 39 years	2,650	30.2	52,262	37,537	26.8	10,127	2,964
40 to 44 years	2,579	35.5	54,891	39,645	29.9	11,606	3,056
45 to 49 years	2,224	36.1	56,072	40,375	26.0	11,674	3,384
50 to 54 years	2,336	37.7	56,279	40,395	29.2	12,479	4,017
55 to 59 years	2,672	40.7	52,621	37,565	34.1	12,766	4,889
60 to 64 years	2,180	33.5	47,153	34,699	25.1	11,506	4,923
65 years and over	4,748	26.9	34,716	28,375	50.0	10,531	5,633

PROPORTIONS AND RELATIVES

	Households		Average Income		Spendable Discretionary Income		
	Number (thousands)	Proportion to households	Before taxes	After taxes	Aggregate (billions)	Average	Per capita
Total	100.0%	100.0	100.0	100.0	100.0%	100.0	100.0
Under 25 years	4.5	66.7	70.2	73.2	2.8	61.2	76.3
25 to 29 years	9.4	83.0	88.9	89.9	6.8	72.7	77.2
30 to 34 years	12.7	110.6	94.7	94.1	10.9	85.7	75.4
35 to 39 years	10.0	96.1	111.8	108.6	9.7	96.2	79.8
40 to 44 years	9.8	112.8	117.4	114.7	10.8	110.3	82.3
45 to 49 years	8.4	114.8	119.9	116.8	9.3	110.9	91.1
50 to 54 years	8.8	119.7	120.3	116.9	10.5	118.6	108.2
55 to 59 years	10.1	129.2	112.5	108.7	12.3	121.3	131.7
60 to 64 years	8.3	106.5	100.8	100.4	9.0	109.3	132.6
65 years and over	18.0	85.4	74.2	82.1	18.0	100.1	151.7

Source: Joint Study, Consumer Research Center, The Conference Board and the United States Bureau of the Census.

the rest of the county, and their homes cost over $200,000, several times the average price for homes in the county.

Local restaurateur Brit Adams is quoted as saying: "It's like somebody came around with a watering can and things just started popping up."

The state government of South Carolina is also making an effort to attract retirees. It recently bought over 3,000 acres of land near a sparsely settled stretch of the Savannah River and plans to build roads and other amenities. The state hopes to interest a developer to build a retirement town for 12,000 people. Local authorities predict that this project will attract 3,400 new jobs. Massachusetts has been acquiring acreage for a similar but smaller development in the northern Berkshires.

When the Exxon Corporation gave up on its oil shale project on Colorado's Western Slope, it was left with a partly developed townsite it had installed to house workers and their families. Management decided that a retirement community offered the best opportunity to recover their investment. According to *The Wall Street Journal*, "The company has changed its model-home plans from big split-levels to smaller, single-story ranch homes, beefed up insulation (warmth was a primary retiree concern), and added a golf course and indoor swimming pool. About 1,500 people have moved in to date."

The potential for outdoor recreation in Michigan's Upper Peninsula and Minnesota's Iron Range (both depressed mining areas), is a major attraction for many retirees, and both areas are trying to market their natural resources. After they lost Reserve Mining Company, the town's major employer, residents of Silver Mine, Minnesota funded an advertising campaign designed to attract new senior residents. The ads, which appeared in far-off newspapers—some ads even appeared in Florida—have already won several dozen retirees who have moved into the area.

After deciding that they couldn't afford the tax abatement, and other incentives that it would take to land the electronics plant that they were after, Bennettsville, South Carolinians changed their target. They are now courting developers of senior housing with the message that the area's rolling countryside would be ideal for golf.

Despite the mounting evidence that when healthy, active and affluent older adults move into town they can rejuvenate the economy, many financially-ailing communities are overlooking the solution that retirees represent, and they continue to chase elusive industries. With a few exceptions, most of the communities enjoying the economic benefits of new retiree residents have stumbled on to the solution by happenstance rather than as a result of serious marketing research.

Some local authorities are buying into the myth of seniors as poor and frail. They fail to recognize the positive economic impact that seniors can have on the community. The successful communities of the future are marketing their best features—safer streets, cleaner air, less crowding and a sense of community—to the active and affluent older Americans seeking the very qualities they offer. They actively solicit older adults, welcoming them to their communities and providing the facilities to accommodate their interests.

For many communities, as well as companies, senior Americans are not the problem, they are the solution.

Spending Patterns

Consumer spending by older men and women is influenced by a blend of individual preferences carried over from earlier life and combined with new kinds of spending that are specific to maturity.

While older persons generally buy the same kinds of things and exhibit similar consumer behavior as younger adults, many of their purchases are motivated by age-related changes in their lives. Changes in the source or amount of income, less work and more leisure, and changes in physical condition and health status are among the major factors that influence the consumer behavior of older persons.

What Older Americans Spend

Average annual expenditures of households, in 1984 dollars	all households	Households Headed by Older Americans			
		total	55-64	65-74	75+
Number of persons in household	2.6	2.1	2.5	1.9	1.6
TOTAL EXPENDITURES	$20,862	$17,144	$22,264	$15,038	$10,718
Food Total	$3,280	$2,900	$3,602	$2,714	$1,865
Food at home	2,300	2,129	2,536	2,027	1,518
Grocery stores	2,164	2,029	2,412	1,929	1,462
Convenience stores	136	99	124	98	55
Food away from home	980	772	1,065	687	348
Housing Total	$6,284	$5,079	$6,195	$4,562	$3,767
Shelter	3,494	2,520	3,124	2,203	1,865
Owned dwellings	2,066	1,526	2,049	1,264	939
Rented dwellings	1,071	641	633	558	781
Fuels, utilities, and public services	1,638	1,645	1,878	1,588	1,292
Household operations	315	275	263	251	332
House furnishings and equipment	837	640	930	520	278
Furniture	270	178	283	119	69
Major appliances	141	123	166	115	56
Small appliances/houseware	62	53	73	49	20
Misc. household equipment	229	169	248	139	66
Apparel Total	$1,107	$788	$1,136	$657	$331
Males, aged 2 and over	285	177	265	140	66
Females, aged 2 and over	447	356	503	307	154
Transportation Total	$4,264	$3,226	$4,435	$2,926	$1,409
Vehicle purchases	1,813	1,247	1,814	1,126	364
Vehicle finance charges	213	113	188	80	25
Gasoline and motor oil	1,058	842	1,134	782	386
Maintenance and repairs	439	344	448	311	197
Health Care Total	$902	$1,256	$1,065	$1,360	$1,458
Health insurance	291	507	329	643	636
Medical services	454	504	524	462	529
Medicines and medical supplies	157	245	211	255	292

Households Headed by Older Americans

Average annual expenditures of households, in 1984 dollars	all households	total	55-64	65-74	75+
Personal Care Total	$192	$203	$243	$195	$139
Personal services, female	121	150	172	149	111
Personal services, males	66	49	66	42	27
Entertainment Total	$973	$674	$1,008	$531	$265
Fees and admissions	313	238	312	226	118
Televisions	219	154	204	131	93
Radios and sound equipment	91	50	92	24	10
Other	350	233	400	149	45
Reading Total	$132	$122	$141	$123	$84
Newspapers	61	71	77	72	57
Magazines/periodicals	33	28	32	29	18
Book clubs	9	7	9	5	3
Encyclopedias/other	3	1	2	1	0
Education Total	$286	$147	$237	$74	$88
Elementary and high schools	46	15	33	3	0
Colleges and universities	175	105	153	60	83
Other	16	10	18	5	2
Alcoholic beverages	$286	$184	$258	$164	$76
Tobacco and smoking supplies	$227	$185	$264	$166	$66
Miscellaneous	$295	$232	$324	$174	$145
Contributions Total	$706	$791	$874	$681	$800
Charities	73	83	79	78	96
Religious organizations	259	303	343	294	241
Educational organizations	13	10	15	7	5
Political	7	12	16	9	7
Personal Insurance Total	$1,928	$1,357	$2,481	$711	$225
Life ins., endowments, annuities	300	297	462	229	90
Retirement/pensions, S.S.	1,628	1,060	2,019	482	134

Source: Bureau of Labor Statistics. 1984 Consumer Expenditure Survey.

And, because they have fewer members in the home, older persons buy less of some items and spend on a different mix of purchases than younger households.

Bureau of Labor Statistics data shows that consumers age 55 to 64 spent significantly *more* than the national average on prescriptions, health and life insurance, fuel oil, home maintenance, small and major appliances, personal care and food at home. This group spent significantly *less* than the national average on rent, mortgage, girls clothing and boys clothing.

Men and women age 65 to 74, a category often referred to as the newly retired, spent significantly *more* than the national average on health insurance, prescriptions, contributions, home maintenance, floor coverings, personal care and food at home. They spent *less* than the national average on education, vehicle finance charges, rent, used cars and children's clothing.

The combination of Social Security, pensions and income from accumulated assets allows the newly retired to maintain a standard of living that is only slightly lower than the preretirement 55 to 64 year group. For the 65 to 74 seniors, increased expenditures show up in insurance, medical services and prescriptions but there is also a marked increase in travel and other discretionary spending. The fact that expenditures for women's clothing and personal care products and services remain constant is a reflection of senior's interest in personal appearance.

The Bureau statistics show that after age 75 consumers spent significantly *more* than the national average on domestic services, home maintenance, medical services, fuel oil, prescriptions and health insurance. Consumers 75 and over spent *less* than the national average on such products and services as furniture, automobiles, clothing, entertainment equipment and sporting goods, shoes and tobacco.

Satisfying Needs

Like all other consumers, seniors buy to satisfy needs. Over forty years ago, noted psychologist Abraham Maslow identified needs and charted them in order of importance. He

Average Annual Expenditures of Urban Consumer Units By Type of Expenditure and Age of Household

Type of Expenditure	Amounts Expended			Percent Distribution		
	Under 65	65-74	75 plus	Under 65	65-74	75 plus
Annual average expenditures	$23,569	$15,873	$11,196	100.0	100.0	100.0
Shelter/furnishings	5,396	3,204	2,661	22.9	20.2	23.8
Utilities	1,718	1,644	1,311	7.3	10.4	11.7
Food	3,603	2,831	1,912	15.3	17.8	17.1
Clothing	1,335	715	346	5.7	4.5	3.1
Health Care	785	1,340	1,487	3.3	8.4	13.3
Transportation	4,838	3,041	1,450	20.5	19.2	13.0
Pension and life insurance	2,358	778	229	10.0	4.9	2.0
Entertainment	1,168	604	291	5.0	3.8	2.6
Cash contributions	1,645	953	632	7.0	6.0	5.6
Other	724	762	878	3.1	4.8	7.8

Source: U.S. Bureau of Labor Statistics. Consumer Expenditure Survey: Interview Survey, 1984. Bulletin 2267, Washington: U.S. Department of Labor, August 1986.

Consumer Expenditures by Type And Age Group: 1984

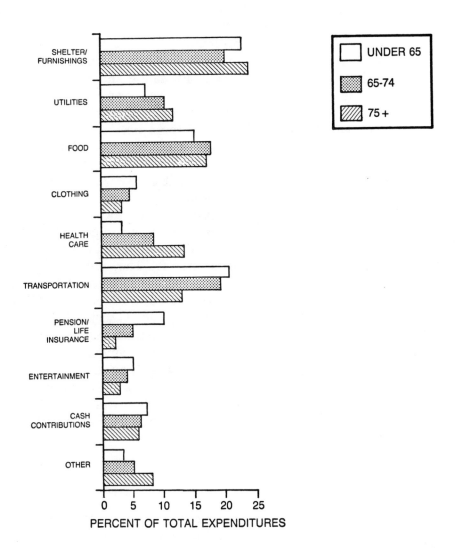

Source: U.S. Bureau of Labor Statistics. Consumer Expenditure Survey: 1984 Interview Survey. Bulletin 2267, Washington: U.S. Department of Labor, August 1986.

concluded that people seek to satisfy needs only after other, more important, needs have been satisfied. It starts with physical and biological needs, such as food, shelter and clothing. Once these basic needs have been met, people will take the next step up the ladder to satisfy safety and security needs, followed by the need for love and affiliation, then, prestige and esteem and finally self-fulfillment needs.

Some products and services fulfill a single need—one buys a burglar alarm specifically for safety and security—while other product and service areas apply across a spectrum of needs. For example, an older individual might travel to satisfy any one or all of these needs. He or she might travel to a health spa to satisfy a physical need, travel to move to a safer area, travel to visit family or a loved one, travel for the prestige and esteem it carries in the community or travel for self-fulfillment.

In dealing with older consumers who tend to be conservative and careful about how they spend their money, the need for prestige, and self-fulfillment are bought only after physical and security needs are met. They will attempt to satisfy a particular need until a more basic need is satisfied, and if a primary need becomes vulnerable, they will forego a higher need until the primary need is secured.

At the same time, it should be noted that mature adults, 50-and-over, are precisely the people most likely to have reached that time in their lives when they can, and do, pursue activities which enhance personal satisfaction and self-fulfillment. This is a characteristic often overlooked by marketers trying to understand the mature market and "what makes it tick."

Grandchildren

It won't be long now before Americans 55 and over will outnumber children aged 15 and under. When that happens at the end of this century, it will be the first time in history that this demographic phenomenon occurs.

Maslow's hierarchy of needs can be adapted to the product and service areas that relate to the life of the older consumer:

Physical and biological needs

Food, shelter, medical care.

Safety and security needs

Insurance, savings, investment, telephone, burglar alarm/security systems, fire alarm.

Love and affiliation

Clothing and personal care products and services to enhance appearance, cosmetic surgery, hair replacement, weight loss, gift purchases, transportation, congregate housing.

Prestige and esteem

Luxury housing, automobiles, clothing, jewelry, country club membership, "gold" credit cards and other conspicuous "status" possessions.

Self-Fulfillment

Travel, post-retirement avocation or work, musical instruments, books, movies, TV, concerts, etc.

So the chances are pretty good that the next senior you meet will have pictures of a grandchild or two on the top of the bureau. The relationship between older Americans and their grandchildren is a very special one. According to a survey of grandparents by *50 Plus* magazine (now called *New Choices*), 46 percent visited their grandchildren 15 or more times in the past year. The survey also finds that 4 out of 10 took a trip with their grandchildren in the past year, and that almost half of the grandparents surveyed called their grandchildren once a week or more. The positive marketing implications of the special relationship that exists between the two generations can be summed up in one word: Gifts.

The number of gifts, and the cost of the gifts, that youngsters receive from grandmother and grandfather are staggering. This is a list of the merchandise bought by grandparents for grandchildren and the percent of the surveyed respondents that bought the item . . .

- Clothing (86 percent)
- Dolls (59 percent)
- Board Games (49 percent)
- Video Games (20 percent)

Consequently, a recent issue of *Grandparents* magazine contained ads for Kids Mart clothing stores, an audio cassette learning program for children 3-to-5 years of age, Red Flyer wagons and other wheeled toys for young children, and the Walt Disney Christmas ornament collection featuring Mickey and the rest of the gang. The editorial matter, with such articles as "Clothes Kids Like to Wear," "The Right Toy Makes a Big Difference" and "Books for Young Readers" supports the advertising and confirms the grandparents interest in such items.

Another magazine, *Grandparent Today* is a closed-circulation quarterly which made its debut early in 1988. It is sponsored by a toy manufacturer, Fisher Price.

The most famous toy store in the world, New York City's FAO Schwartz has been quick to capitalize on the largesse of grandparents. They've opened "The Grandmother Shop" which features such sentimental items as handmade blankets and comforters, expensive rattles, handmade satin booties and other gift items for the silver-spooned offspring of affluent parents and grandparents.

Even the hospitals have gotten into the act. St. Paul Medical Center in Dallas offers grandparent classes. For a $10 tuition fee, grandparents are given a quick course on the latest in new-born baby care.

By catering to the demands of free-spending seniors, American enterprise can tap into two major trends and their consequences—the baby boomers are having babies and their parents have become proud and generous grandparents.

Out-Of-Pocket Health Costs

The major threat to the financial security of older persons in the U.S. is the high out-of-pocket cost of health care. Older persons spend more on health care in actual dollars, and as a percentage of their total expenditures than younger people. Households with a reference person age 65 to 74, paid $1,487 in out-of-pocket health costs in 1984, versus $785 paid by younger households. The major health expense for older urban households in 1984 was health insurance; the major health expense for younger households was for hospital and doctor's bills.

Even with fewer people at home, older Americans spent over three times as much as their young counterparts on health insurance ($625 versus $202), and twice as much on prescription drugs and medical supplies ($261 versus $128). There was little difference in the patterns of health expenditures, for households headed by people 65 to 74 and people 75 and over, from the pattern for older households as a group.

PART TWO
THE MESSAGE

"Your magazine is beginning to depress the daylights out of me. Do you realize there are those of us in our 60's who smoke, drink, dance, exercise, golf, travel and work, who do NOT have diabetes, high cholesterol, high blood pressure or arthritis? I wish you'd lighten up your ads and articles and consider us."

A female reader from Salem, Oregon, in a letter to the editor of Modern Maturity

CHAPTER THREE

SHAPING THE MESSAGE

Why is so much general advertising clever, imaginative and effective, while advertising aimed at the older generation continues to be dull, stereotype ridden and ineffective?

Writing in *Fortune* magazine, Eleanor Johnson Tracy concedes that "The market poses excruciating challenges for advertisers. Boldly confronted, age can be a turnoff. Advertisers don't want to offend the old by calling attention to advancing wrinkles and other less pleasant manifestation of aging. Nor do they want to alienate the young by focusing on the old. So far not many advertisers have found the magic formula."

There is, of course, no magic formula. But to succeed in reaching the mature consumer one must come to grips with a paradox: The market is defined by age, but the marketer who uses age as the sole basis for planning marketing strategy and shaping the advertising message misses the point and ultimately misses the target. Age is only one dimension in classifying consumers—and not necessarily the most important one. Other factors such as health, finances, lifestyle (active vs. passive), mobility, work status, marital status, living arrangement, etc., often outweigh age as a qualifiers of consumer potential.

The lifestyles and consumer behavior of our older generation is changing rapidly, and it is difficult to gain perspective on change while it is happening. How else does one explain why so much of the advertising addressed to seniors is condescending, insensitive and out of touch with reality?

There is more art than science in creating good advertising, and there are certainly no absolutes in creating advertising to attract the attention—and the dollars—of older Americans. The ideas and suggestions that follow, integrated with sensitivity and good judgment, will help you construct an effective approach to the mature market.

As outlined in Chapter 1, much of consumer behavior is based on perceived age rather that actual age. The message to marketers is clear: When you talk to seniors take off 10 to 15 years. Target your message to the perceived age rather than the chronological age. And when you portray seniors in ads or TV commercials, show them as positive and active people, looking and behaving the way people look and act at the perceived age.

The older person (retired or otherwise) is not shelved away from mainstream society; put seniors where they really are, in contemporary settings and environments. In your next senior market ad, scuttle the lace curtains and bring in some decorator vertical blinds. Too often the portrayal of older adults and their surroundings is based on outdated images rather than reality.

Aging does not necessarily mean disabled or frail. Most older adults today are healthy, active and mobile, thanks to improved medical care, interest in fitness and nutrition. Ads should reflect the independence and vitality of today's senior population.

Modern Maturity magazines's guidelines for advertisers contains valid clues for reaching the older consumer: "We stress positive messages, and decline ads that take negative approaches. For example, the analgesic ads we publish are those that suggest, 'Feel great with . . .' We regretfully decline those that say, 'I feel terrible—give me an . . .' We decline ads featuring words such as pain, inflammation, suffer, hurt, ache, and flare-up. We also tend to avoid anatomical graphics dealing with analgesics or other products." Aside from being more upbeat, this approach encourages advertisers to address the older person more realistically; that is, as a whole person, not just the sum total of his aches and pains.

In Pursuit of an Age-Irrelevant Society

There are several good reasons why it is important to avoid age-marking your product or service and your ads. From a practical point of view, age-marking a product or service limits the market across a broad spectrum of ages without gaining any additional acceptance from the targeted age group. For all enlightened Americans trying to promote the concept of an age-irrelevant society, labelling a product or service by age, is a giant step backward.

Blatant reference to age can also be a turn off: nobody likes to be pigeonholed. Seniors will resist products or services designed for "old people." They don't want to be seen purchasing products labelled by age or "senior," and they don't want age-labeled products around the house for visitors to see.

Mature adults don't want to be segregated in a world of age peers. Ads and commercials are most effective when they portray believable interaction between the sexes and between generations. Ads should show older men and women as they really are—part of the crowd.

The changing roles of men and women in our culture has had its impact on the older generation as well. Many mature women hold important jobs and many older men shop for groceries and tend the garden. Ads which recognize this fact of later life would be a refreshing change and are sure to be noticed.

Substance, Credibility and Quality

Brevity has its place in advertising but not in messages designed for senior consumers. These are veteran shoppers—they've been shopping for many years. They want the full story spelled out. Seniors have the time and the patience to analyze and evaluate your message. This is particularly true when marketing a new product or service. They are interested in trying new products and new ideas, but they need to be convinced and their attitude is strictly, "I'm from Missouri, you've got to show me." You've got to give them detailed reasons for trying something new. Relate new information to something familiar. Familiar product demonstrations and line extensions of well-known brands help to create acceptance of the new. Whether you're marketing an established product or service or something brand new, whenever possible back up your promise to seniors with hard facts—the guarantees, the warrantees, the official endorsements and the test results.

Don't insult the intelligence of an experienced consumer by exaggerating the benefits or promising more than you can deliver. After a lifetime as a consumer, and getting stuck once or twice, mature adults can spot an offer too good to be true.

Ads that are clear and straightforward win the confidence of the older consumer. With this market, audio and visual overload can be a costly mistake. Loud, fast-paced and wise-guy ads and commercials that may work for other age groups turn them off. Seniors prefer advertising with a familiar structure and an unambiguous message.

More than any other group, seniors want substance, not glitter. As seasoned shoppers, they want value for their money and they recognize quality when they see it. Stress quality. They appreciate and are willing to pay for quality.

The transition to seniority is a learning experience and there are things that seniors want to know. They will respond to ads that are chock full of information relevant to their stage of life. Provide information that helps them to keep fit, manage their money, enhance their life satisfaction and cope with personal problems and to become knowledgeable counsellors providing advise for others. Despite the stereotypes that say otherwise, seniors are receptive to new ideas and new products, they welcome change if it means change for the better.

Celebrity Spokesmen

Celebrities, particularly the veteran performers, are part of the senior world. They are part of their past, they reflect their values and they are models for a productive, highly visible way of life in later years. Having a product promoted by a recognized personality can create a unique affinity with the consumer. Because seniors are avid television viewers, TV personalities become part of the family. People feel that they know them even though they've never met or actually seen them in person.

The ad agencies are aware of the advantages of having a known and respected personality deliver the message and they use celebrities as spokesmen and as endorsers of products and services. Ed McMahon, Martha Raye, Elizabeth Taylor, Danny Thomas, Art Linkletter, Tennessee Ernie Ford, Karl Malden, Robert Young, Patricia Neal, Lauren Bacall, Dick Van Dyke, and Bob Hope are some of the personalities currently appearing in advertisements and commercials targeted at the mature. Each brings to the advertising message the recognition and credibility that make for successful endorsement advertising.

Lighten up

There's a great deal of laughter and fun in the lives of older Americans and ads should reflect that aspect of the senior world. Many of the pressures of their earlier lives are lifted and they are now ready and able to enjoy life. Portray them in happy situations, surrounded by friends, children and grandchildren. Show seniors with a smile on their faces. Your ad should smile along with them.

The best ads addressed to seniors are those that involve the prospect by telling a story or with light humor. Illustrations and photographs that create a sense of recognition with their own life and problems are particularly effective. (Chinese proverb: Tell me and I'll forget, show me and I may remember, involve me and I'll understand.)

Seniors like good food, they enjoy cooking and they are good cooks. Many men who were busy earning a living and doing other things in their earlier years, become pretty good cooks in their later years. They are nutrition conscious and seek out low salt, low fat foods but they still enjoy the things they grew up with—corn flakes, Oreo cookies, hot chocolate and ice cream. So, don't assume that all older customers exist solely on bran and eat alone. Show them eating with others and entertaining. Many take great pride in feeding family and friends generously.

Give the cliches a rest. Pass up the stock photos of seniors playing shuffleboard and gramps-going-fishing, seniors are also involved in the more active sports. Of course, their interests aren't only related to leisure and recreation. Older men and women in your advertising should also have productive, occupational identities. Many formally retired individuals are still actively engaged in important, useful work and will relate to the productive older person more readily than to the playful retiree stereotype. In these instances, the nature of the product will help determine the tone of the ad.

Keep in mind that there's more to the mature years than just surviving. That means satisfying relationships and yes, romance. Clothes, cosmetics, fitness and everything else that helps seniors look and feel attractive and maintain their sexual identities are important. Stress the intangibles. Portray older adults enjoying positive experiences and living their days and nights to the fullest.

Advertising to Seniors

Special communications and advertising techniques are required when marketing goods or services in personal categories which reflect the physical, psychological and behavioral differences in the age groups. Such categories would include, for example, fashion, apparel, personal care, over the counter medicines, and travel. In most other categories, good advertising that works for the general public will work just as well for seniors, so don't think you necessarily have to create a special ad for the mature market. You can reach your target by placing the ad in a senior publication or by placing your commercial next to a program with an older audience.

Studies show that word of mouth is a major source of information for older men and women and they have an informal communication network that works. Advertising that is informative, relevant and provocative starts the word of mouth going.

Marketers should also be aware of the mechanical aspects of creating an ad or commercial for the senior market. For example . .

- Use large type.

- Don't use reverse type for large amounts of body copy. It's more difficult to read.

- When possible, include a toll-free 800 number or some other way to order or get more information easily. Make response convenient. Cutout coupons should be easy to get at.

Senior Models

One of the signs of stepped-up mature market activity is the increased demand for older models, both men and women, for print and TV advertising and for catalog work. This is a recent phenomenon. In the past, popular models were dropped from consideration when the first wrinkle appeared. Lyman Clardy, a well-known model, says he was dropped by his model agency when he reached 50 and other models report similar experiences of losing work when they grew too old to satisfy youth-seeking casting directors and ad agency art directors.

Now Lyman Clardy is signed with New York model agency, Rogers and Larman, which has established a "Senior Class" division to meet the demand for older models. Working with his new agency, Clardy is in constant demand and makes several thousand dollars a shoot playing a doctor, a chairman of the board and other professional types.

In reference to older models, David Roos, president of Gilla Roos model agency reports that "Products from Coca Cola to insurance companies are paying more attention to them." His "real people" agency makes a specialty of providing silverhaired models.

In fact, the three leading model agencies in New York—Ford, Elite, and Rogers and Larman report an increase in requests for older models in recent years. Maria Theresa Zazzara, the head of the Classic Women Division of the The Ford Model Agency says, "Increased demand is putting it mildly. The market for older models has exploded in the last year." She credits the success of Lears magazine as a breakthrough in making maturity respectable and says, "The models that would have been asked to retire 10 years ago are not anymore." Models booked at Ford's Classic Women Division (age 40 and over) have appeared in upscale ads for BMW automobiles, Debeer's Diamonds, Epson Computers, and Harrah's Marina Resorts.

While Zazzara sees the greatest increase in requests for her Classic Women in fashion catalogs but she also anticipates increased work for older models in TV commercials and print advertising.

To capitalize on the increased demand for older models, Elite, another large New York model agency, formed its own special division, "Elite Elegance," which provides models in older age categories.

AT&T and Canon Copiers are major clients of Rogers & Lerman's "Senior Class" division which books men and women, 50 and over, as models for both consumer and trade advertising. Peter Lerman, the model agency's head reports that while the demand has increased for older models, it is not quite equal to the increased percentage of older people in the population. He believes that advertisers need to more realistic about the real source of their business: "You watch those Cadillac commercials on television where they have men and women in their thirties. You know and I know that men and women in their thirties don't buy Cadillacs. They're completely missing their market."

A great deal of the ambivalence that marketers display in dealing with older customers is evident in the advertising of cosmetics and skin care products. Do you advertise wrinkle fighting salves and creams by showing a twenty year old model who may face the problem in the future . . . or a fifty year old model fighting the wrinkle battle now?

When Germaine Monteil, a cosmetics company owned by Revlon, had to make this decision, the first model the company chose was a twenty year old. They wanted to reshoot the ad with a model who looked 35 or 45 years old and really concerned with wrinkles but the ad ran with a model who was at most in her twenties. "Some companies are dancing around the age issue and others seem to be avoiding it altogether," says Linda Wells, a writer on beauty for the *New York Times*.

Oil of Olay has chosen to tackle the age issue without equivocation. Their ad shows a woman who could be thirty saying, "I don't intend to grow old gracefully. I intend to fight it every step of the way." Neutrogena's ad campaign of "real women" (i.e., not models), has actress Nanette Fabray revealing her age as "over 60." Commenting on the Neutrogena campaign, Wells said, "The women are attractive, but realistic: some have crow's feet, some laugh lines, and some even think about getting older."

Neutrogena may be one of the few cosmetic companies that represent the older woman attractively. Other companies and their advertising agencies are still grappling with ways to talk about wrinkles without showing them. Barbara Feigin, a Grey Advertising Agency executive who has studied consumer attitudes on aging concedes, "This is tricky stuff. Everybody is unnerved about it. The tradition in the past has been so youth-driven. It's hard to change those patterns. But if you look at the change in the population, you realize you have to change or get left in the dust."

Mature Marketing Professionals Needed

"Marketers interested in reaching older Americans have enormous misconceptions about their attitudes and purchasing habits," says Donnelly Marketing.

The conclusion is based on a study sponsored by Donnelly, which compared the response of consumers, over age 50, with the responses of professional marketers. Richard J. Balkite, Donnelly's director of senior marketing, said, "The differences are striking. While business is clearly aware of the importance of targeting the changing needs, desires and lifestyles of consumers over the age of 50, marketers are woefully lacking in an understanding of what they are. I would call it 'the 28-year old brand managers syndrome' except that it seems to apply to senior management as well."

Some of the highlights of the survey's findings reinforce Balkite's point:

- Older Americans rate themselves more active, both physically (53 percent) and mentally (83 percent) than the professional marketers rate them.

- Twice as many mature consumers are interested in trying new brands, products and technologies (52 percent) as marketers think (27 percent).

- Five times as many older consumers spend more in supermarkets now (compared to when they were younger) than marketers think (27 percent).

- More than one-third of consumers, age fifty and over, are interested in automobiles, exactly the same number as in the younger age bracket surveyed. Professional marketers guessed that only one-fifth would be interested.

As Balkite suggests, many of the people creating and marketing new products and services are themselves young to middle-aged. They are more attuned to the interests, needs and preferences of people their own age. It's a clear case of marketing by the young to the young. Today's youthful marketing professionals in their thrities and forties do not have, nor should they be expected to have, a visceral feel for the psyche of the older person. With the increased size and formidable spending power of the mature market, industry cannot afford to depend solely on the marketing judgment of young men and women.

In response to this need, marketers are adding older man and women to their marketing team. On a full or part-time basis, or as consultants to management, veteran marketers provide the intuition and sensitivity needed to relate successfully to the mature consumer.

Instructive Failures

Nobody said it was going to be easy. Several firms went courting the mature consumer only to be rebuffed along the way. Their failure is our lesson.

Gerber Foods, a well-known maker of baby foods, observed that many older men and women were buying baby foods and concluded that they needed simple food because they wore dentures, or had digestive problems, and were buying the baby foods for their own consumption. Gerber brought out Senior Citizen, a food product with the same easy-to-eat, easy-to-digest qualities as the baby food. It proved to be a major marketing error and was quickly removed from the market. Labeled as "baby food" the checkout clerk and everyone else observing the purchase could think it was meant for a grandchild, but an age-labeled jar stigmatized the purchaser. The same senior who gladly accepts the "senior citizen discount" at the movies will avoid age-labeled products that are a constant reminder of their age and carries a label for all the world to see.

Affinity shampoo hoped to capture a lucrative niche by advertising itself as a shampoo "for hair over age 45." Knowledgeable marketers would tell them, albeit in retrospect, that women don't want to be confronted with their age every time they wash their hair. Affinity is not forever—the shampoo is no longer on the shelf.

Attitudes of Elderly Customers
Survey Examined Attitudes of Consumers 50 Years and Older

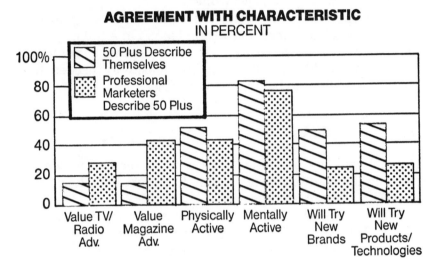

AGREEMENT WITH CHARACTERISTIC
IN PERCENT

The famous Wendy's "Where's the Beef?" television commercial, achieved notoriety but insulted many older viewers who felt that Clara Peller's performance created an image of old people as cranky, eccentric and somewhat daft.

Oldsmobile has always enjoyed great popularity with older car buyers. A full size car, it's comfortable and reliable—qualities that seniors prefer in an automobile. However, Oldsmobile was stigmatized by the age association, to the point where even older drivers deserted the car because they didn't want to be seen driving an "old man's car." General Motors has launched one of the biggest advertising campaigns in history to erase the stigma and establish "a new generation of Olds." The ad copy says, "This is not your father's Oldsmobile. This is a new generation of Olds."

Percent Interested in Goods and Services

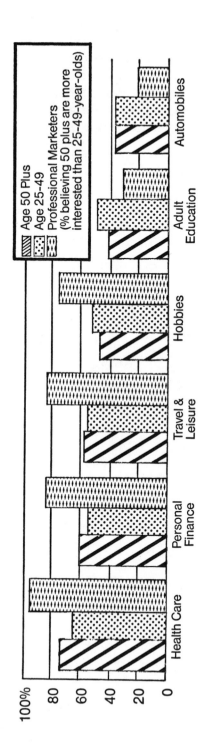

Source: *Washington Post*, based on Donnelly Marketing Survey.

Let's not repeat some of the errors of predecessors. What's in the head and heart is more important than the number of candles on the cake. We can help make America an "age irrelevant" society by selling the benefits that seniors value without age-marking our product or service.

CHAPTER FOUR

SELECTING THE MEDIA

In order to measure the relative use of the different media by various age groups, Simmons Market Data categorized adults into five groups based on the frequency of their use of media. Heavy users were defined as those falling into the highest user category, the top 20 percent.

Simmons finds that older individuals are avid TV viewers. About 32 percent of people 65 and older and 24 percent of people 55 to 64 are heavy television watchers compared to 15 percent of people 18 to 49.

The highest proportion of heavy newspaper readers is among the 55 to 64 year olds, and the percentage of heavy newspaper readers among people 65 and older is slightly higher than it is among the better educated 18-to-49 segment of the population.

While older individuals are not among the heaviest magazine readers, they read certain magazines (*Readers Digest*, for example) in greater numbers and with greater frequency than younger adult readers. They are, of course, frequent readers of "senior" magazines like *Modern Maturity* and *New Choices* (formerly *Fifty Plus*) which are published specifically for their age group.

Radio and outdoor advertising are usually directed at ·young consumers, but radio has much to offer mature market advertisers. Radio is local, relatively inexpensive

81

and good for targeting age segments with specialized programming.

Television Viewing

More and more these days, one sees television programming and advertising directed at the older viewer. Among the TV shows most popular among men and women 55+ are "Golden Girls," which celebrates the lifestyle of the three active and unmarried older women relocated in Miami, and "Murder She Wrote" starring 66-year-old Angela Lansberry as a writer of mystery novels and each week features different mature TV and film stars in cameo roles.

The emphasis on health, nutrition and other subjects of particular interest to older viewers on the morning and evening network news shows, indicates a serious effort to attract seniors. Commercials for high-bran breakfast cereals, expensive Lincoln automobiles and the latest anti-wrinkle skin balms (mostly products with high brand name recognition) during prime time and for retirement housing developments, local HMOs, health care facilities and health insurance on local stations during odd hours indicate how advertisers, large and small, are using the media to reach seniors.

While there are no television stations with programming exclusively for seniors, there are times when you would think you're watching just such a station. An informal monitoring of commercials on CBS during four Sunday evening hours reflects the way senior-targeted commercials are clustered.

Here are the commercials that ran during the four-hour period that showed "Sixty Minutes," "Murder She Wrote" and a made-for-TV movie: an airlines commerical advertising its "Get Up and Go Passport for Seniors." (The theme: "It's Your Turn.") Followed by a commercial for Sealy Posturepedic Mattress. Followed by the AARP soliciting memberships. That was followed by Oil of Olay. (The theme: "Why Grow Old Gracefully?")

And then in quick succession, Polident Powder, Cadillac automobiles (advertising itself as "a good investment"); next a remedy for gas pains, then Sears Discover Card, followed by a commercial for Keopectate and a frozen food product with 25 percent less fat, salt and calories. The next commercial featured the beautiful 71-year old Lena Horne talking about Post Cereal, followed by Oldsmobile with the tag line, "a whole new generation of automobiles."

This TV time period has virtually been taken over by advertisers trying to reach a mature adult audience. We can expect to see more such clusters of TV time devoted to older viewers.

The increase in the amount of programming and advertising directed at senior viewers is a recognition of the simple fact that older Americans watch a great deal of television, more than most other age groups. While the viewing habits of older persons in general, reflect the general viewing patterns of all adults, a study by The National Council on the Aging (NCOA) based on viewing diaries obtained by Simmons Market Research, finds a variance from the norm in that TV viewing by older persons is particularly high during the daytime hours. During the early morning, 7 a.m. to 9 p.m., roughly 12 percent of adults 55 and older watch television. For the period 9 a.m. to 1 p.m., this rises to 13 percent for adults 55 to 64 and 18 for adults 65 and older. According to the NCOA study, television viewing increases during the afternoons with 22 percent of adults 65 and older, and 17 percent of adults 55 to 64.

Like adults in other age categories, older individuals increase viewing dramatically during prime time and prime time fringe periods, times when the differences between older and younger groups are the smallest. In early prime time, between 7:30 and 8:00 p.m., 52 percent of adults 65 and older, and 44 percent of adults 55 to 64 watch television. The rate climbs to 46 percent of adults 55 and over during prime time, 8:00 to 11:00 p.m. In the late prime time fringe, 11:00 to 11:30 p.m., the audience shrinks to about 36 percent of adults 65 and older and 35 percent of adults 55 to 64. In the late evening, 11:30 p.m. to 1:00 a.m., the proportion of older adults who watch TV drops to about 10 percent.

Advertisers seeking cost-efficient ways of reaching the mature TV viewers should consider daytime slots which attract a high proportion of older viewers. While persons 55 and over represent only a third of all adults, they account for 45 percent of early morning viewers, 44 percent of mid-morning viewers and 40 percent of those who watch in the afternoon. Health care advertisers seeking compatible programming should be aware that the morning hours are crammed with news and talk shows which feature health topics in both local and national programs.

Television is, without a doubt, the most effective advertising medium in history. The results of the audio and visual impact of television transmitted to millions of consumers at one time are awesome. For mature market advertisers, the results can be improved substantially when the commercial appears within or next to programming of particular interest to older viewers. That's the good news. The bad news is that it costs a fortune and that places it out of reach for many marketers. Of course, it is possible to use less expensive advertising by running locally produced and transmitted commercials, but they reach a smaller audience and the choice of time slots is limited.

Radio Advertising

Radio is the domain of the young, the very young. Almost half of all adult radio listeners are 18 to 34 years of age. But with the growing awareness of the size and income of the senior market, radio stations are shifting their programming to appeal to older audiences and attract advertisers trying to reach that audience. To accomplish this, radio stations are increasing the amount of time allotted to News, Talk, Classical Music, Easy Listening and Nostalgia formats, and some stations offer programming exclusively in one or several of these areas.

Because the bulk of its audience is so young, radio defines the mature audience as younger than other media do. In fact, when a group was set up to create promotional material that radio stations would use to develop their mature market business, the group called itself "The 35-Plus Committee." This group's presentation to the advertising world entitled, "The Amazing Invisible Market," defined the older market as 35 to 64. In the rock-and-roll world of contemporary radio, old age starts at 35 and people over 64 simply don't exist.

Radio promoters are selling their product short. People age 35 are not part of the mature market, and older people over 64 make up a substantial part of the radio audience. Radio defines the older segment of the population by their musical tastes and programming preferences, rather than by their numbers, needs and purchasing power. They forget that seniors started out in life years before TV, at a time when there was only radio. They like radio and would listen a great deal more if the program content was more in line with their interests.

While roughly 45 percent of the adult audience is 18 to 34 years of age, and only 20 to 25 percent of the radio audience is comprised of adults 55 and older, resourceful use of radio can still be an effective way to reaching mature listeners. Nearly 55 percent of the 55 to 64 set listen to radio in the early morning—drive time for commuters—and 48 percent of those 65 and older listen to the radio in the early morning.

Low production and broadcasting costs make radio an interesting possibility for establishing name and brand recognition, or to sing the praises (literally!) of a local merchant. The number and variety of local radio stations available in most areas allow advertisers to target their message to older adults. Radio offers mature-market advertisers a cost-efficient combination of reach, frequency, and formats that interest seniors. Adults 55 and older account for 47 percent of the listening audience of news/talk stations and 42 percent for all-news stations, compared to 29 percent of the audience for other contemporary stations.

However, since radio is limited to brief audio messages it is not the ideal medium when time is needed for a full explanation or when visual images are needed to convey the advantages of the product or service. Radio is often a

Daily Adult Television and Newspaper Usage

Daily Adult Television and Newspaper Usage

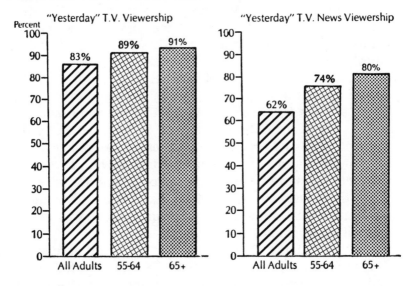

Daily Adult Newspaper Readership

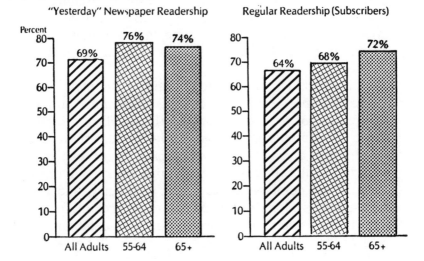

Source: Newspaper Advertising Bureau.

poor producer for direct response advertisers. Many listeners are driving, eating, cooking or doing something else when listening to the radio and it's·just not convenient to respond in writing or by phone.

Magazines

People read newspapers for local information; they read magazines because they are interested in the range of subject matter featured in the publication. For mature-market advertisers, magazines offer an opportunity to reach seniors and to segment, by interest, groups within the mature market. (*Prevention* magazine, for example, has a large number of senior readers with a particular interest in health and fitness.)

While national magazines may not be a practical medium for smaller or local advertisers, many magazines now have regional editions in the larger metropolitan areas. It gives small-budget, image-seeking advertisers the prestige and interest group of a major magazine at a lower cost. In recent years, regional magazines, offering both geographic concentration and upscale reach, have become an important advertising medium for reaching affluent older adults.

Magazines are not as ephemeral as newspapers; they have a way of staying around for awhile. Magazine advertisers have been known to get response from magazine ads many months after publication—from the dentist's office, probably.

Readers Digest is read by 29 percent of adults 55 and older. A large portion of the magazine's readership is in that age group and the editorial content of the magazine includes subjects of particular interest to mature readers. *TV Guide* and *People* are also read by a substantial number of seniors, but readership in both of these general interest magazines is higher among younger people, and the editorial content reflects this fact.

Many women's magazines are widely read by older women. Better than 20 percent of women 55 to 64 read *Family Circle, Good Housekeeping, Women's Day* and *Better*

Homes and Gardens. These magazines attract women 65 and older as well. For magazines with a large readership of older men, look to *Popular Mechanics* and *Field and Stream*. The news magazines: *Time, Newsweek* and *U.S. News and World Report*, are an important source of information for many mature consumers. Studies show that 13 percent of adults 55 to 64 and 8 percent of adults 65 and older read *Time* regularly. Advertising space in *National Geographic* is very expensive but effective in reaching an older audience.

Older individuals form the bulk of *Prevention* magazine's readership. Approximately 7 percent of women 55 to 64 and 4 percent of women 65 and older read the magazine. Almost 24 percent of *Prevention* readers are 65 or older, and 22 percent are 55 to 64.

Many new magazines devoted specifically to the mature interests of seniors have emerged in recent years. These publications provide older adults with information and ideas relevant to their stage of life and provide advertisers with effective channels of communication to their targeted mature market.

Listed below are some of the major senior magazines that accept advertising.

Modern Maturity   A monthly magazine with a circulation of 22.4 million, this is far and away the primary publication for reaching the senior market. The American Association of Retired Persons (AARP) is the publisher and subscription is automatic with association membership. With membership growing at 8,000 new members every day, *Modern Maturity* recently overtook *TV Guide* to becomes the largest circulation magazine in the U.S. A special edition of the magazine is published for the members of the National Retired Teachers Association The editorial content of all editions includes a wide range of subjects directed at senior interests with emphasis on travel and career, financial planning, the arts, beauty and fashion, social life and world affairs.

Advertising rates for *Modern Maturity* are among the highest in the nation. A full page, four-color ad is priced at $218,215; full page, black and white is priced at $196,940. Partial circulation and 12 regional editions, with rates reduced accordingly, are also available. There is a 10 percent discount on national advertising for publishers, travel services and non-profit organizations.

In addition to being high-priced, the magazine has stringent guidelines for the advertising it will accept. They "tend to exclude ads which lump older persons into one category—especially ads characterizing older persons as sick, feeble, infirm, deaf or confused." In keeping with this policy, and for reasons of balance, the magazine excludes ads for products such as wheelchairs, laxatives, denture adhesives and hearing aids, and maintains numerical quotas on such product categories as over-the-counter drugs, mail order shoes and health publications.

Advertising offices for *Modern Maturity* are at 420 Lexington Avenue, New York, N.Y. 10017. 212 599-1880.

New Choices: For The Best Years This is a new name for an established magazine, *50 Plus*, which was recently purchased by the Reader's Digest Association. Associate publisher Richard Thorne says that the new name was chosen because "this age group is at a time in their life when they are facing many choices." Management felt that the original name narrowed the field by being too age specific and expects to see the average age of its readers (now 62) dropping with the new, less age-specific name.

Subscription fee for *New Choices* is $15 per year and the current circulation is 575,000. Along with the name change, the magazine has broadened its editorial content to include features on travel, finance and lifestyle. The cost of a full page, four-color ad is $22,000; full page black and white is $16,160.

For additional information call or write *New Choices*, 28 West 23d Street, New York, N.Y. 10010.

Golden Years In its tenth year of publication and now national, it started as a regional magazine in Florida. (Florida, with 3.9 million seniors, leads the nation in senior population percentage—19 percent. The sunshine State's age ratio is considered a microcosm of the composition of the U.S. population at the end of the century.) The magazine is directed at what it calls the "ideal model matrix" magazine reader: a (predominantly) female reader between the ages of 55 and 64, with a household income of $40,000+, who is college educated and travels extensively.

At the time it went national, *Golden Years* had a controlled circulation in Florida of 180,000. Full national circulation is 400,000. The objective is to convert to paid subscription and larger readership. A four-color full page ad in *Golden Years* national edition is $15,290; full page black and white, $11,880. Advertisers can buy full Florida editions or any one of three regions in Florida.

Golden Years is located at 233 E. New Haven Ave., P.O. Box 537, Melbourne, Florida 32902-0537. 407 725-4888.

Lear's . . . which carries the subtitle "For the woman who wasn't born yesterday," started publishing in February of 1988 and appears to be an early success. The magazine is edited for "the sophisticated, educated, affluent woman over 40." Seventy five percent of its readers are between 40 and 64 and almost 10 percent are 65 and over. Median household income of its readers is $75,000, and over 60 percent of its female readers are employed.

Lear's is a slick, up-scale magazine which exudes glamour and affluence, and reflects the personality of Frances Lear, its owner founder. Current advertisers read like a "who's who" in providers of luxury and elegance. The magazine published 10 issues in 1989 and published monthly starting in 1990. Rate base circulation is 450,000; 80 percent subscription, 20 percent newsstand. A full page four-color ad is $22,433. Retail stores, direct by-mail ads, individual hotels and resorts, schools, publishers and real estate advertisers are offered a 20 percent discount.

The magazine's advertising office is at 655 Madison Avenue, New York, NY 10021, 212 888-0007. Publishers representatives for *Lear's* are also in Detroit and San Francisco.

Mature Outlook . . . is distributed to members of the Sears sponsored club of the same name for adults 50 and over. It is published bimonthly, and page rates are $18,060 for color and $16,255 for black and white. Average age of readers is about 60.

For additional information contact Meredith Publishing, 1716 Locust Street, Des Moines, Iowa 50336. 515 284-3050.

Connections ... A four-color magazine published six times a year, guarantees a 300,000 mailed circulation which goes to affluent older persons, almost all of whom have taken at least one trip in the past year; more than half have an income of $30,000 and over.

It is published by Saga International Holidays, Ltd., a tour operator for men and women age 60 and over.

For additional information on circulation profile and advertising rates, contact *Connections*, 120 Boylston Street, Boston, MA 02116. 617 451-6808.

Other magazines directed specifically at a mature readership which accept advertising include ...

Active Senior Lifestyles 411 Washington Avenue, Minneapolis, MN 55401. 612 349-6901. Circulation, 30,000.

Indiana Horizons Media Management Group, 5563 W. 73d Street, Indianapolis, IN 46268. 317 298-7100. Circulation, 300,000.

Senior Life 1420 E. Cooley Dr., Colton CA 92324. 714 824-6681 Circulation, 30,000 in Southern California.

Renaissance 143 Newberry Street, Boston, MA 02116. 617 262-4515 Circulation, 200,000. Distributed by banks to affluent 55+.

Second Wind 15 Ketchum Street, Westport, CT 06880. 203 226-7463 Circulation, 160,000.

Longevity 1965 Broadway, New York, NY 10023-5965. 212 496-6100 Circulation, 200,000.

The Best Years   A Sunday supplement to The New York Times, 229 W. 43d Street, New York, NY 10036. 212 556-1196. Circulation, 1.2 million.

Grandparents Today   Cahners Publishing, 475 Park Avenue S., New York, NY 10016 212 545-5353. Circulation 1.5 million.

December Rose   J.E. Publishers Reps., 6855 Santa Monica Blvd. Los Angeles, CA 90038. 213 467-2266. Circulation 200,000 (22 States).

Access Chicago   1500 Shermer Road, Northbrook, IL 60062. 312 498-9828. Circulation, 50,000.

Retired Officer   201 N. Washington St. Alexandria, VA 22314 703 549-2311. Circulation, 356,000 retired military.

McCalls Silver Edition   230 Park Avenue, New York, NY 10169. 212 551-9571. Circulation, 1. million. 6 × Year, McCalls insert.

Memories   Diamandis Communications, 1515 Broadway, New York, NY 212 719-6056. Circulation, 600,000. Quarterly.

New Years   1729 Grand Avenue, Kansas City, MO 64108. 816 234-4215. Circulation, 166,000. Magazine supplement in Kansas City Star.

Retirement Life   1533 New Hammshire, NW, Washington, DC 20036 202 234-0832. Circulation, 500,000 retired government employees.

Newspapers

Local newspapers, daily or weekly, allow advertisers to target communities with a large senior population. They are especially important in promoting local businesses and services. The special-interest sections of the daily paper help in reaching specific groups—the business section is traditionally read by older men while food sections featuring recipes and meal ideas and the gardening section have a larger readership among older females. Some newspapers have periodic health and fitness supplements and they usually attract older readers.

The cost of newspaper advertising, relative to magazine or television advertising, is low and most newspapers offer reduced advertising rates for frequent insertions. The lower cost of newspaper advertising makes it possible to buy enough space to explain a product fully. When a product or service requires a detailed explanation, this can be a tremendous advantage.

When looking for a direct response from potential customers, newspaper advertising is the medium of choice. Most people won't hesitate to clip a response coupon from a newspaper or make a quick telephone call to a number listed in the paper. The fact that a newspaper is "today" is both a strength and a weakness. It's timeliness means prompt readership and response; it also means that, unlike a magazine, it won't be around tomorrow to catch the reader who missed the advertisement before.

In its publication, "Channels of Communication for Reaching Older Americans," the National Council on the Aging reports that older Americans are avid newspaper readers, and cites the following data to support that claim: Nearly 74 percent of adults 55 to 64 read a daily paper and 72 percent read a weekend paper. About 69 percent of people 65 and older read a daily paper and 62 percent read a Sunday newspaper.

Newspaper magazine supplements are particularly effective in reaching older consumers. Nearly 71 percent of adults 55 to 64, and 62 percent of adults 65 and older read a weekend paper and most Sunday newspapers contain a magazine supplement with editorial content aimed at senior interests. Parade, a popular, nationally-syndicated magazine supplement, is read by 45 percent of adults 55 to 64 and 37 percent of adults 65 and over.

Several networks sell advertising in regional senior publications on a group or multiple purchase basis. A single insertion order can place advertising with any one or several publications within a network, allowing advertisers great flexibility in advertising costs and regional focus. Leonard J. Hansen, the head of Senior Publishers Group, one of the largest of the senior newspaper networks and a pioneer in the development of senior newspapers, calls it "the fastest growing publishing field in the country."

According to Mr. Hansen, the senior newspaper "is the trade journal of the retiree". He believes that senior papers have produced outstanding results for advertisers because they are read thoroughly and referred to often: "Virtually everything in the senior newspaper is pertinent to seniors and almost 90 percent of the content is not available to the older reader through other media."

Senior newspapers are usually tabloid format and published weekly or monthly. Senior newspapers run the gamut in the way they are distributed—paid mail, free mail, audited, paid controlled or free controlled, free door-to-door.

Senior Publishers Group is comprised of newspapers and magazines written, edited and published for active and affluent older adults (55+). Established in 1977, this organization represents 98 local and regional newspapers and magazines serving the mature market in the U.S. and Canada with a total circulation of over four million readers. One insertion order/one invoice advertising placement in any of the senior publications listed below is available through Senior Publishers Group, 1326 Garnet Avenue, San Diego, California 92109. Phone (800) 727-3646 or (619) 272-9023.

Publication, Geographic Area, Circulation

Senior World,   San Diego, California, 100,000.

Senior World,   Orange Country, California, 100,000.

Seniors Chronicle,   San Clemente, California, 24,300.

Leisure World News,   Laguna, California, 11,509.

Leisure World,   Gold Coast Combo, California, 111,684.

Leisure World,   Saddleback Combo, California, 51,639.

Golden Rain News,   Seal Beach, California, 9,000.

California Senior Citizen,   Los Angeles, California, 63,000.

Senior World,   West Los Angeles, California, 100,000.

Senior World,   Los Angeles, 100,000.

Senior Highlights,   South Coastal, California, 110,000.

Senior Highlights,   Central Coastal, California, 100,000.

Senior Highlights,   Inland California, 40,000.

Senior Highlights,   COMBO, 250,000.

CA Senior,   San Luis Obispo and Santa Barbara, California, 50,000.

Senior News/Views,   Sonoma and Marin Co., California, 25,000.

Golden State Mobilehome,   California, 90,000.

Maturity Monthly,   North Los Angeles, Kern, California, 57,000.

Leisure Life,   Sun City, Hemet, California, 30,000.

Valley Messenger,   Yucaipa, California, 15,800.

Senior World,   Central Coast, California, 40,000.

Maturity Monthly,   Fresno, California, 30,000.

The News,   Santa Cruz, California, 12,500.

California Federal Retiree,   Statewide California, 56,000.

Maturity Magazine,   Canada, 212,000.

Prime Time,   Seattle, Washington, 15,000.

The Messenger,   Vancouver, Washington, 14,500.

Senior Times,   Spokane, Washington, 25,000.

Senior Power,   Spokane, Washington, 10,000.

Third Age,   Snohomish Co., Everett, 15,000.

Retirement Life News,   Portland, Oregon, 65,000.

Senior Tribune,   Portland, Oregon, 50,000.

Prime Time,   South Coast, Oregon, 9,500.

Senior News,   Willamette Valley, Oregon, 46,000.

Senior Views,   Grants Pass., Oregon, 15,000.

Idaho Senior New,   Idaho, 9,800.

Arizona Residence Group,   Valley-Sun, Arizona, 150,000.

Arizona Winter Visitors (Oct-Apr),   Arizona, 20,000.

Green Valley News,   Green Valley, Arizona, 8,200.

Cracker Barrel,   Tucson, Arizona, 25,000.

Senior Times,   Las Vegas, Nevada, 2,500.

Senior Beacon,   Colorado, 75,000.

Senior Edition,   Denver, Colorado, 30,000.

Senior Edition,   Special Report, Colorado, 50,000.

Senior Voice,   Wyoming, Colorado, 25,000.

Golden Age,   Utah, 1,500.

Conquest,   Greater Detroit, Michigan, 387,000.

Senior Voice,   Tuscola, Huron, Michigan, 2500.

Mature American,   N. Detroit, Oakland, 20,000.

Mature American,   Milwaukee, Wisconsin, 20,000.

Senior News,   South Bend, Indiana, 4,600.

Senior Beacon,   Greater Indianapolis, 20,000.

Senior Beacon,   Southwest Kansas, 10,000.

Active Aging,   Wichita, Kansas, 40,000.

Senior Citizen News-Views,   Chicago, Illinois, 68,000.

Senior Courier,   Rockford, Illinois, 27,000.

Senior Citizen News-Views,   Cleveland, Ohio, 30,000.

Senior Citizen News-Views,   Akron, Ohio, 30,000.

Senior Citizen News-Views,   Peoria, Illinois, 25,000.

Senior Citizen News-Views,   Dubuque, Iowa, 30,000.

Prime Time,   SCN&V, Mt. Pleasant, Iowa 25,000.

Prime Time,   Quad Cities, Iowa, 23,000.

Iowa Senior Times,   DesMoines, Iowa, 10,000.

50 Plus Lifestyles,   DesMoines, Iowa, 35,000.

New Horizons,   Nebraska, 32,000.

Maturity Monthly,   Fox Valley, Wyoming, 30,000.

Maturity Monthly,   COMBO, 42,000.

Senior Life,   Fort Wayne, Indiana, 35,000.

Senior Life,   South Bend, Indiana, 35,000.

Chicago Senior American,   Chicago, Illinois, 500,000.

Federal Retiree,   Florida, 21,000.

Senior Voice,   Penellas, Florida, 36,100.

Senior Citizen News-Views,   Orlando, Florida, 60.

Mature Lifestyles,   St. Petersburg, Florida, 40,000.

Gulf Coast Senior Beat,   Sarasota, Florida, 27,000.

Senior Citizen News-Views,   Ft. Meyers, Florida, 40,000.

Florida Senior Times,   Jacksonville, Florida, 20,000.

Senior Voice,   North Carolina, 14,000.

Senior Tribune,   Atlanta, Georgia, 21,500.

Mid-South Senior,   Memphis, Tennessee, 27,000.

Senior Sentinel,   Nashville, Tennessee, 15,000.

Active Lifestyles,   Nashville, Tennessee, 50,000.

Senior Views,   South Louisiana, 20,000.

Silver Years News,   Bellaire, Texas, 25,000.

Senior News,   Corpus Cristie, Texas, 20,000.

Active Age,   Arkansas, 20,000.

SR Dallas,   Texas, 54,000.

Golden Times,   Wayne, New Jersey, 32,000.

Senior New-Views,   Erie, Pennsylvania, 26,000.

Senior Views,   Pittsburgh, Pennsylvania, 85,000

The Elder,   New Haven, Connecticut, 10,000.

Senior News,   Long Island, New York, 25,000.

Senior Voice,   Nassau County, New York   Senior Beacon, New Hampshire, 20,000.

Senior Advocate,   Worcester, Massachusetts, 20,000.

Carriage Trade,   Boston, Massachusetts, 21,643.

Senior Times,   Boston, Massachusetts, 50,000.

Prime Time News,   Baltimore, Maryland, 17,500.

Fifty Five Plus,   Maine, 20,000.

Maine Say,   Maine, 20,000.

Seniors USA,   National.

Retirement Money,   National.

Senior Spectrum Newspapers publishes tabloid newspapers for seniors ("a vital information source for people 55 and older") in Northern and Central California and Northern Nevada. Eighteen editions with a combined circulation of 250,000 (600,000 readers claimed) serve major markets in these regions. Editorial content includes legislative developments, travel, health, personal finance and community matters. Senior Spectrum newspapers consist of both paid and controlled circulation delivered via second and third class mail. Management says that one of their newspapers, *The Sacramento Weekly,* is the largest all-paid newspaper in the field.

Senior Spectrum Newspapers can be reached at 9261 Folsom Blvd., Suite 401, Sacramento, California. Telephone (916) 364-5454.

Region (W=weekly, B=bi-monthly, M=monthly), Circulation

Sacramento, W, 25,000
Stockton, W, 14,000
Redding, B, 7,000
Chico, B, 10,000
Fresno, M, 18,000
Modesto, M, 10,000
Bakersfield, M, 10,000
Solano, M, 10
San Francisco, M, 15,000
San Mateo, M, 17,000
Alameda, M, 17,000
Contra Costa, M, 17,000
Santa Clara North, M, 17,000
Santa Clara South, M, 24,000
Marin, M, 10,000
Sonoma, M, 16,000
Monterey, M, 10,000
Reno, M, 10,000

Senior Media Network   represents 16 senior newspapers targeted "to affluent older Americans," with a combined network circulation of 934,475. It is based at 2207 South 48th Street, Tempe, Arizona 85282, 602 438-1566.

Newspaper, Area Covered, Circulation

Arizona Senior World,   Metropolitan Phoenix and Tucson, 125,000.

Senior Life,   San Diego, CA, 30,000.

Senior,   San Luis Obispo and Santa Barbara, CA, 48,000.

Desert Community Newspapers,   Palm Desert, Palm Springs and Indio, CA, 83,075.

Senior Times/Mobile Home World,   San Jose, Santa Clara and Santa Cruz, CA, 53,000.

Rossmoor News,   Rossmoor and Contra Costa, CA, 6,400.

Nevada Senior World/Senior Times,   Nevada, 25,000.

Retirement Life News,   Portland OR, 65,000.

Golden Age,   Salt Lake City UT, 35,000.

Active Senior Lifestyles Magazine,   Minneapolis and St.Paul, MN, 30,000.

SR Dallas (Prime Times),   North Dallas TX, 50,000.

Ohio Legion News,   Ohio, 148,000.

Senior Times,   Columbus OH, 20,000.

Senior Times,   Southwestern PA, 46,000.

Senior News,   Long Island, NY, 25,000.

Golden Times,   Rochester, NY.

Direct Marketing

Any type of direct-to-the-consumer sales effort is part of direct marketing. Mail advertising, the most important component of direct marketing, is effective, targeted and cost-efficient advertising. Direct mail also has the virtue of allowing for a longer message; the advertiser has as much space as he needs to explain, to describe, to show, to persuade and to solicit the order. Unlike the mass media, it provides total control over quality and content.

Direct mail is particularly effective for certain age-related services because it allows the advertiser to reach a receptive prospect with ultimate timing precision. For example, purveyors of health insurance to supplement Medicare benefits (sometimes referred to as Medigap), can time their mail communication, or telephone solicitation, to reach the individual two or three months before the prospect's 65 birthday, when he or she becomes eligible for Medicare. If the prospect is approached at the time such a purchase is being considered and a decision must be made before the birthday arrives, the likelihood of a sale is very high. The success of this technique has been proven by the life insurance industry. For many years, life insurance marketers have been timing their solicitation to coincide with crucial birthdays.

In addition to timing, the other crucial components in any direct mail advertising campaign are copy, design, and, most important of all, the mailing list. Assuming the need for your product or service and assuming its superiority in meeting that need, nothing is as important in acquiring the desired results as the quality of your mailing list. Unless you are familiar with mail lists and mailing-list suppliers, you would be surprised at the number and variety of lists of mature adults that are available to advertisers.

On page 106, you'll find a roster of companies that specialize in the category known in the industry as "senior citizen" lists. If you can't find a list that precisely matches your requirements, with the large number and variety of types available it's likely you can come close.

Other direct marketing activities, which have proved useful to advertisers in reaching for the mature market, are television commercials and radio and magazine ads where consumers are required to write or call in their order. Telephone solicitation or "telemarketing" and catalog sales have also produced outstanding results with this market.

James R. Lumpkin, a marketing professor at the University of Mississippi, reports that in a recent six month period, of those making at least one direct-selling purchase, 51 percent were 65 or over. Of the total older population segment study, 17 percent made direct purchases.

Direct selling, as distinguished from direct marketing, involves personal selling and home demonstration—party sales, door-to-door selling, etc. It is worth noting that 56 percent of those age 65 and over have made purchases using direct marketing, compared to only 17 percent for direct selling.

Only 34 percent of the sample group made no direct marketing or direct selling purchase in the six month period under study, and over 60 percent made at least one purchase in response to a direct-marketing solicitation.

Older consumers were not found to differ greatly from younger consumers in the frequency of their direct marketing purchases, but according to Professor Lumpkin, when they did respond they spent a great deal more per order. Direct mail was once a vehicle for selling only low cost merchandise. This is no longer true. Upscale retailers and catalogs with high priced items (Neiman Marcus, Sharper Image, L.L. Bean) are scoring great success with direct mail and many items in these catalogs are aimed at older, well-heeled consumers. A recent Gallup survey found that purchasers over age 50 are the most likely prospects for gourmet food items sold through the mail.

The kind of demographic analysis that leads to successful marketing starts with a profile of the customers for a product or service. Such a profile should reveal the age range of customers, their income and family status. Once you have a firm grasp of this information, you can search out concentrations of customers who match this profile. A high-potential concentration can be be localized to a specific geographic area, or it can be scattered throughout a general area that is easy to reach through direct mail advertising.

There is no one way to create a valid customer profile; they come in different forms and from different sources. Sometimes it's personal knowledge, a retailer who "knows" his customers. Profiles can be constructed from customer surveys or customer purchase records. If this isn't available, a profile can be created by running a series of demographic reports around your best locations and using this data as a benchmark customer profile. CACI, a market and analysis research organization in Fairfax, Virginia specializes in creating profiles and in matching profiles. Such information can be used for any number of purposes—retail site selection, identifying segments of the market that are the best prospects for a particular product or service, real estate development, and measuring market penetration to name a few.

The services of CACI, and other such demographic analysis firms, are used extensively by direct-mail marketing firms. Firms that sell through direct mail know very little about their customers—sometimes just their address. According to CACI, demographic analysis can "facilitate the inference of much information about customers from very little data." With the profile created through demographic analysis, direct mail advertisers can select the best match (those most likely to respond to a specific solicitation) from the billions of names available for purchase or rental.

Retailers, banks or service providers that deal with consumers are likely to have lists of customers by name and address. Demographic analysis uses these lists, relates them to specific neighborhoods and assigns a code for that neighborhood. In this way, a geodemographic profile of your best customers can be constructed, and that profile can be used to fine-tune your list selection to target areas where you are seeking more customers.

Customer profiles can also help to improve advertising effectiveness in such areas as media analysis and selection, direct response, telemarketing, product positioning and creative strategy. For each kind of media—TV, radio, newspapers, magazines, etc.—you can compare your customer profile with the media profile, and target customers according to which TV shows they watch, to what radio formats they listen and at what time of day, the frequency with which they read newspapers, and which magazines they read.

On pages 107 to 110, you'll find a demographic analysis of such a study of the "55 PLUS" residents in a hypothetical town. It contains a wealth of information broken down by incremental age segments within the senior population. It also provides forecasts to a specific future year (1993 in this example), and data on income and household value. This is the kind of information that is the foundation for a successful mature-market campaign.

Direct Mail Lists

The most recent edition of Standard Rate & Data's volume of direct mail lists contains a separate section on "Senior Citizen" lists. It describes over 85 different suppliers of direct mail lists with names and addresses of mature consumers, in quantities ranging from several hundred thousand to several million. It gives the conditions of rent or purchase, amount of names available, source of names, breakdown by age, year in which the list is compiled, etc.

SOURCES OF SENIOR CONSUMERS MAILING LISTS

LM = List Manager
LO = List Owner
LC = List Compiler

Market Compilation and Research Bureau, Inc. 11633 Victory Blvd, North Hollywood, CA 91609 LM
    Buyers and renters of medical equipment.

ABC - Advanced Business Compilation, 223 Main St., Port Washington, N.Y. 11050 LC
    Accredited Well-To-Do Senior Citizens

BFC Mailing Lists, Inc., 1900 Quail St., Newport Beach, CA 92660 LC
    Doners to National Committee to Preserve Social Security and other organizations, all 50+.

Senior Citizens Marketing Group, Inc., 9319 LBJ Freeway #120, Dallas, TX 75243
    Senior citizens by exact age and home residence.

Lead Marketing International, Inc., P.O. Box 932, Denton TX 76202 LC
    Affluent senior consumers 65 and over.

(continued on page 111)

"55 PLUS" Chart 1

```
                          55 PLUS                    PAGE 1 OF 4

ANYTOWN, USA            AREA REFERENCE:        RADIUS: OUTER   4.00
4TH & ELM STREET          LATITUDE:   38 52 10 DEGREES NORTH  38.87
0 - ANY SIZE RADIUS       LONGITUDE:  77  9 20 DEGREES WEST   77.16

                    1980      1988      1993    1988-1993   ANNUAL
                    CENSUS    ESTIMATE  FORECAST  CHANGE     GROWTH

POPULATION          261511    282890    285439    2549        0.2%
HOUSEHOLDS          109725    125901    131927    6026        0.9%
AVG HH SIZE           2.33      2.20      2.12   -0.08       -0.7%
MEDIAN AGE           32.1      37.3      39.3      2.0        1.1%
MEDIAN HH INC $     23489     41750     49039     7289        3.3%
PER CAPITA INC $    11559     19807     23296     3489        3.3%
-------------------------------------------------------------------

                          AGE BY SEX

MALES          1980            1988              1993

          Number % of 55+  Number % of 55+   Number % of 55+

55-59       6812     31.1     6494    24.3      6917    24.2
60-64       5861     26.7     6245    23.4      6046    21.2
65-69       3960     18.1     5650    21.1      5531    19.4
70-74       2718     12.4     4036    15.1      4655    16.3
75-79       1407      6.4     2376     8.9      3001    10.5
80-84        706      3.2     1254     4.7      1521     5.3
85+          455      2.1      673     2.5       885     3.1

Total      21919    100.0    26728   100.0     28556   100.0


FEMALES        1980            1988              1993

          Number % of 55+  Number % of 55+   Number % of 55+

55-59       8190     26.0     7290    19.3      7534    18.8
60-64       7347     23.3     7587    20.1      7114    17.8
65-69       5347     17.0     7582    20.1      7180    18.0
70-74       4158     13.2     5961    15.8      6911    17.3
75-79       2833      9.0     4140    11.0      5147    12.9
80-84       1918      6.1     2854     7.6      3283     8.2
85+         1752      5.6     2326     6.2      2823     7.1

Total      31545    100.0    37740   100.0     39992   100.0


TOTAL          1980            1988              1993

          Number % Tot Pop Number % Tot Pop  Number % Tot Pop

55+        53464    20.4    64468    22.8     68548    24.0
65+        25254     9.7    36852    13.0     40937    14.3
75+         9071     3.5    13623     4.8     16660     5.8
85+         2207     0.8     2999     1.1      3708     1.3

-------------------------------------------------------------------
COPYRIGHT 1988 CACI, FAIRFAX, VA
```

"55 PLUS" Chart 2

AGE OF HOUSEHOLD HEAD BY INCOME

1980 Number of Household Heads

HOUSEHOLD INCOME IN THOUSANDS	55 +	65 +	75 +	55-64	65-74
Under $15	9361	6433	2855	2927	3579
$15 to $24.9	6847	3314	954	3533	2360
$25 to $34.9	5174	2161	480	3013	1682
$35 to $49.9	5688	1908	297	3780	1611
$50 to $74.9	3457	876	131	2581	745
$75 and over	1155	366	51	789	315
TOTAL	31682	15058	4768	16623	10292
Median $	24464	18307	12525	31145	21640

1980 Percent Distribution

HOUSEHOLD INCOME IN THOUSANDS	55 +	65 +	75 +	55-64	65-74
Under $15	29.5	42.7	59.9	17.6	34.8
$15 to $24.9	21.6	22.0	20.0	21.3	22.9
$25 to $34.9	16.3	14.4	10.1	18.1	16.3
$35 to $49.9	18.0	12.7	6.2	22.7	15.7
$50 to $74.9	10.9	5.8	2.7	15.5	7.2
$75 and over	3.6	2.4	1.1	4.7	3.1
TOTAL	100.0	100.0	100.0	100.0	100.0

"55 PLUS" Chart 3

AGE OF HOUSEHOLD HEAD BY INCOME

1988 Number of Household Heads

HOUSEHOLD INCOME IN THOUSANDS	55 +	65 +	75 +	55-64	65-74
Under $15	6122	4779	2512	1344	2266
$15 to $24.9	5345	3793	1555	1551	2239
$25 to $34.9	5632	3388	1189	2243	2199
$35 to $49.9	6389	3478	932	2910	2547
$50 to $74.9	7453	3553	721	3900	2833
$75 and over	7762	3134	548	4629	2585
TOTAL	38703	22125	7457	16577	14669
Median $	40288	32351	22823	51542	38713

1988 Percent Distribution

HOUSEHOLD INCOME IN THOUSANDS	55 +	65 +	75 +	55-64	65-74
Under $15	15.8	21.6	33.7	8.1	15.4
$15 to $24.9	13.8	17.1	20.9	9.4	15.3
$25 to $34.9	14.6	15.3	15.9	13.5	15.0
$35 to $49.9	16.5	15.7	12.5	17.6	17.4
$50 to $74.9	19.3	16.1	9.7	23.5	19.3
$75 and over	20.1	14.2	7.3	27.9	17.6
TOTAL	100.0	100.0	100.0	100.0	100.0

AGE OF HOUSEHOLD HEAD BY INCOME

1993 Number of Household Heads

HOUSEHOLD INCOME IN THOUSANDS	55 +	65 +	75 +	55-64	65-74
Under $15	5293	4234	2388	1059	1847
$15 to $24.9	4689	3449	1644	1239	1805
$25 to $34.9	5257	3492	1477	1765	2014
$35 to $49.9	7001	4130	1412	2871	2718
$50 to $74.9	7290	3888	1059	3401	2829
$75 and over	11700	5301	1156	6399	4145
TOTAL	41230	24494	9136	16734	15358
Median $	46518	38893	28629	60534	46109

1993 Percent Distribution

HOUSEHOLD INCOME IN THOUSANDS	55 +	65 +	75 +	55-64	65-74
Under $15	12.8	17.3	26.1	6.3	12.0
$15 to $24.9	11.4	14.1	18.0	7.4	11.8
$25 to $34.9	12.8	14.3	16.2	10.5	13.1
$35 to $49.9	17.0	16.9	15.5	17.2	17.7
$50 to $74.9	17.7	15.9	11.6	20.3	18.4
$75 and over	28.4	21.6	12.7	38.2	27.0
TOTAL	100.0	100.0	100.0	100.0	100.0

"55 PLUS" Chart 4

HOUSING VALUE BY AGE OF HOUSEHOLD HEAD

1980 Number of Household Heads

HOUSING VALUE IN THOUSANDS	55 +	65 +	75 +	55-64	65-74
Under $50	1011	523	156	488	367
$50 to $74	4178	2154	573	2024	1580
$75 to $99	6974	3135	769	3839	2366
$100 to $124	3238	1268	340	1970	928
$125 to $149	1797	746	84	1050	663
$150 to $199	1212	487	61	725	426
$200 and over	475	165	43	310	122
TOTAL	18885	8478	2026	10406	6452
Median $	90248	87456	84233	92524	88514

1980 Percent Distribution

HOUSING VALUE IN THOUSANDS	55 +	65 +	75 +	55-64	65-74
Under $50	5.4	6.2	7.7	4.7	5.7
$50 to $74	22.1	25.4	28.3	19.5	24.5
$75 to $99	36.9	37.0	38.0	36.9	36.7
$100 to $124	17.1	15.0	16.8	18.9	14.4
$125 to $149	9.5	8.8	4.1	10.1	10.3
$150 to $199	6.4	5.7	3.0	7.0	6.6
$200 and over	2.5	1.9	2.1	3.0	1.9
TOTAL	100.0	100.0	100.0	100.0	100.0

---

1. INCOME FIGURES ARE EXPRESSED IN CURRENT DOLLARS FOR 1980 AND 1988. 1993 FIGURES ARE EXPRESSED IN 1988 DOLLARS.

2. DUE TO REGIONAL DIFFERENCES IN HOME VALUE PRICE ESCALATION SINCE 1980, ANY ADJUSTMENTS IN THE DATA SHOULD BE BASED ON TRENDS IN HOME VALUES WITHIN YOUR TRADE AREA.

Sources of Senior Consumers Mailing Lists (Continued)

Generation Marketing, Inc., 1 Lincoln Plaza, New York, NY 10023 LC
Individuals by exact date of birth.

CPS Direct Marketing Inc., 7822 S. 46th St., Phoenix, AZ 85044 LM
Ambassador mail order buyers, 95 percent female, by age.

Prescott List Management, 17 E. 26th St., New York, NY 10010 LM
Buyers through American Health Service senior citizen catalog.

Senior Citizens Unlimited, 711 Westchester Ave., White Plains, NY LC
Older adults in 900 cities, compiled from public records.
Lists of 65 and over seniors who requested health insurance information.
Seniors who recently moved, compiled from public records.

American Fund Raising Lists, 600 Winter St., Waltham MA 02154 LC
Charitable donors, 75 percent male, average age 58.

Qualified Lists Corp., 135 Bedford Rd, Armonk, NY 10504 LM
Members of Catholic Senior Citizens Association, age 50+.

The Listworks Corp., 40 Radio Circle, P.O. Box.459, Mount Kisco, NY 10549 LM
Members of Association of Informed Senior Citizens.

American List Counsel, Inc. 88 Orchard Rd., Princeton, NJ 08540 LM
Mail order buyers, available by age segments.

List Services Corp., P.O. Box 2014, 890 Ethan Allen Hwy., Ridgefield CT 06877 LM
Donors to health and political appeals.
List of members of senior discount club.

Phillips Publishing, Inc. 7811 Montrose Rd., Potomac mD 20854 LO
Subscribers to Cardiac Alert newsletter, 70 percent men. "Retirement Edens" bookbuyers

CBS Magazines, 1515 Broadway, New York, NY 10036 LO
Magazine subscription expires, by age segments.

Cromwell Lists, 4944 Commerce Parkway, Cleveland OH 44128 LM
Do-It-Yourselfer Database, mail order buyers, by age.

Doubleday Mailing Lists, 501 Franklin Ave., Garden City, NY 11530 LO
Age-coded book club members, 80 percent female.

Executive Services Companies, P.0. Box 851918 Richardson TX 75085 LC
Demographically selectable Americans, 50+, 65+.

Woodruff-Stevens & Assoc., 345 park Ave. So., New York, NY 10010 LM
Subscribers to "50 Plus" magazine, average age 62.3

Modern Handcraft, 4251 Pennsylvania Ave., Kansas City, MO 64111 LM
Gardening magazine subscribers, average age 58.

The Specialists, 120 E. 16th St., New York, NY 10003 LM
Mail order buyers of gardening equipment, by gender and age.

Prescott List Management, 17 E. 26th St., New York NY 10010 LM
Mail order buyers of vitamins, health products, 55+.

Action Markets, 1710 Highway 35, Ocean, NJ 07712 LM
Ad and direct mail response, 50+, 65+, 70 percent male.

Lifestyle Selector, 1621 18th St., Denver CO 80202 LC
Grandparents, new and dated lists.
Lifestyle segregated lists of seniors available.

NCRI List Management, 45 Legion Dr., Cresskill, NJ 07626 LM
Insurance Data Bank 50+, demographic breakdowns available.
Retirees, Mail order merchandise buyers.

Johnson Direct Marketing, 200 E. 7th St., Loveland, CO 80537 LO
Retired consumers, 50+ and older age segments available.

Hanover House, 340 Poplar St, Hanover PA 17333 LO
Mail order buyers, 50+, 70 percent female.

Madison Direct Marketing, 295 Madison Ave., New York, NY 10017 LC
Individuals over age 50.

Metromail Corp., 360 E. 22d St., Lombard IL 60149 LC
Computerized list, 50 to 64, 65 and over.

Response Marketing, 9 Hunts Lane, PO Box 518, Chappaqua, NY 10514 LM
Hearing aids inquiries, most 55+.
Health insurance inquiries, median age 55.

5M List Company, 2525 Wilson Blvd, Arlington VA 22201 LO
Members of National Alliance of Senior Citizens.

Demographics Systems, 325 Hudson St, New York, NY 10013 LC
Grandparents, selections by date of birth available.

Blue Chip List Representatives, 70 Riverdale Ave. P.0. Box 4565, Greenwich, CT 06830 LM
Mail order buyers of products for 50+, 80 percent female.

Adco List Management Svcs., 333 N Michigan Ave., Chicago IL 60601 LM
Buyers and inquiries, medical appliances.

Compuname, Inc., One Penn Plaza, New York, NY 10119 LM
Subscribers to "Prevention," health magazine, 73 percent
female.

Fred Wolf List Co, 280 N Central Ave., Hartsdale, NY 10530
LC
Large lists of retired people at home addresses.

R.L. Polk & Co., 6400 Monroe Blvd., Taylor, MI 48180
Large lists of seniors, retired people, etc.

Customized Mailing Lists, Inc. 1906 Field Road, P.0. Box 20878,
Sarasota, FL LC
Retirees, seniors; breakdown by college-educated
available.

DSI List Management, 325 Hudson St., New York, NY 10013
LM
Mail order buyers of retirement publications.

Donnelly Direct, P.0. Box 10250, 70 Seaview Ave, Stamford CT
06904 LC
Large lists of seniors, breakdown by lifestyle available.

Advanced Management Systems Inc., 9255 Sunset Blvd., Pent-
house, Los Angeles, CA 90069 LM
Senior's inquiries on insurance products, 60+.
Lists of widows residing in Florida.

Senior Spectrum Inc., 9261 Folsom Blvd. #401, Sacramento CA
95826 LO
California "Senior Spectrum" subscribers, 55+.

Steve Waxman Mailing Lists, 3 West End Ave., P.0. Box 402,
Old Greenwich CT LM
Inquirers about retirement housing in sun belt states.

21st Century Marketing, 4 Dubon Ct., Farmingdale NY 11735
LO
Mail order buyers age 50 and over.

Modern Handcraft, 4251 Pennsylvania Ave., Kansas City MO 64111 LO
Subscribers to home arts magazine, median age 55.

Zeller & Letica Inc., 15 E 26th St., New York, NY 10010 LO
Lists of senior citizen centers and services.
Seniors 55+, age and affluence breakdowns.

Age Marketing, 2255 Ridge Rd., Rockwell TX 75087 LC
Seniors 55-64, high income segments available.

Metromail Corp., 360 E. 22d St., Lombard IL 60148
Americans over 50, 60 percent male.

Focus Marketing, 1900 Quail St., Newport Beach CA 92660 LM
Donors to preserve Social Security and Medicare.

Rubin Response Management Services, 3315 Algonquin Road, Rolling Hills IL 60008 LM
Mail order respondents to health insurance offer, 60 percent male, available by age segments.

Lead Marketing Intnl. P.O. Box 932, Denton TX 76202 LC
50+, exact age selections available.

RMI Direct Marketing, 4 Skyline Dr., Hawthorne, NY 10532 LC
50+, breakdowns by age, income, etc.

Senior Power Pack, Kelley Advertising, 3320 E. Shea Blvd., Suite 195, Phoenix, AZ 85028 Phone: (602) 996-1166
Publishes a foil-wrapped card pack containing the ads of individual advertisers. Mailed three times a year to 100,000 older adult households (55+) in the metropolitan Phoenix area.

For more detailed information on these companies and other available lists, refer to . . .

Standard Rate & Data
Mailing Lists Red Book
National Register Publishing Co.
3004 Glenview Rd.
Wilmette, IL 60091

For additional sources of mailing lists, refer to . . .

Directory of Mailing List Houses
B. Klein Publications
P.0. Box 8503
Coral Springs FL 33065

National Mailing List Houses
(Small Business Bibliography 29)
Small Business Administration
P.0. Box 15434
Ft. Worth TX 76119

Outdoor Advertising

If you're advertising a local service with a message that can be stated briefly (in a phrase or a sentence), consider outdoor advertising. It is relatively inexpensive, but can be highly effective if strategically placed near your location and at a place where it will be seen by older men and women. Some outdoor advertising locations, ads on benches near a bus shelter, for example, are particularly appropriate.

For billboard advertising, location is the prime consideration. The billboard should not only be highly visible, but in a general environment consistent with the product or service being promoted.

Yellow Pages

Yellow Pages advertising is the most logical and pragmatic medium available. It is read by people with the clear intention of purchasing a product or service and at the time they expect to act on their decision. In his book *Advertising Health Services*, Trevor Fisk points out that "about 1 in every 10 patients uses the Yellow Pages as at least one source in deciding which doctor to use."

As an ongoing reference for people who are actively seeking a specific product or service, the Yellow Pages are almost an obligatory advertising medium.

CHAPTER FIVE

TECHNOLOGY CREATES MATURE MARKET OPPORTUNITY

The great growth industry of the 1990s—catering to the needs and desires of America's aging population—will be spearheaded by technology and by academia, government and business working together to find new solutions to old problems. The designers, manufacturers and service innovators who harness technology to serve mature adults will find a highly receptive and lucrative market for their products and services.

The insatiable needs of the large and growing number of mature adults create both challenge and opportunity for enterprising individuals and companies. New drugs and surgical procedures are needed to lengthen the lifespan and improve the quality of the later years. Improved communication systems are required to facilitate preventative care and enable older adults to take greater responsibility for their health. Progress in organ transplants and in the development of life-sustaining machines would contribute to longevity and change the demographics for decades to come.

Technology has also created mature market business

opportunities in areas other than health and medical care. It has provided industry with the tools to satisfy the growing demand for new senior living environments and for advanced computer-driven communications to make it easier for older adults to shop, handle their banking and keep in touch with the world. Developments in the use of electronic robots in industry create working conditions conducive to older workers—they do the blue-collar heavy work allowing workers to shift to service activities, and making it possible for older workers to remain on the job and be productive longer.

Demographics tell us that there is a vast number of mature consumers and they have the spending power to purchase goods and services which will improve the quality of their lives. Technology, which is defined as the development of knowledge and its application to solving practical tasks and problems, can refer to bio-medical research in arthritis as well as wheelchairs used by people with arthritis. Technology can be "soft" (research and knowledge), or "hard" (products and services resulting from research), "high" (complex) or "low" (simple). In all its forms, and in the many areas of senior living that it touches, technology provides business with unprecedented opportunities to give mature customers what they want.

New products range from "low technology" products such as oversized zipper pulls and AT&T's big button phones, to "high technology" instruments such as cardiac pacemakers and kidney dialysis machines. New and innovative mature market services range from heart surgery and organ transplants, to "Medigap" health care insurance to help pay for such costly and sophisticated treatment. In a less crucial area, but one gaining in importance among seniors seeking to regain their youthful appearance, are a number of cosmetic surgery procedures including eye, breast and belly lifts.

Once designers and manufactures recognize the financial incentives that exist in accommodating the mature market, we'll see a constant flow of attractive and functional products leaving the factories and entering the marketplace.

Medical Technology Breakthroughs

Purveyors of eyeglasses and contact lenses are among the industries enjoying record sales as a direct result of the aging population. Most older adults experience some form of reduced vision. Eyeglasses in single vision, bi-focal and even tri-focal lenses (with invisible demarcation lines for the sake of appearance), as well as hard, soft and disposable contact lenses, are helping millions of older adults improve their vision. Eyeglasses have become as much a fashion statement as a remedy for anything less than 20/20 vision. Seniors have joined the rest of the population in their willingness to pay premium prices for "designer" eyeglasses.

Major eye problems associated with the later years, such as glaucoma and cataracts, are spotted early by private eye-care clinics and surgery facilities that have captured a large part of the market from single-practice eye surgeons. Unlike practicing eye surgeons, the clinics have become aggressive and sophisticated marketers, reaching out to its patients by conducting free eye examinations wherever older adults congregate. One such organization, Health Management Services of Chicago, conducts free eye care screenings for seniors at community centers, banks, and libraries.

Companies that offer solutions to the hearing problems that often accompany the later years are similarly positioned to participate in the dynamics of aging America. Approximately 70 percent of the hearing impaired are over age 50, but only about 15 percent actually wear a hearing aid. Many seniors resist wearing a hearing aid because the large bulky earpieces stigmatize the wearer. Thanks to technological strides in this field, hearing aids have become smaller, to the point where they are practically invisible. New types of hearing aids built into the temples of eyeglasses serve two problems at once—vision and hearing. Beltone, the nation's largest manufacturer of hearing aids, is an example of a company that has flourished catering to the needs of older adults.

The high cost of medical services creates a demand for products which enable seniors to monitor and treat themselves. One such instrument, a Blood Pressure Monitor, enables individuals to monitor their own blood pressure. There are several easy-to use models on the market with such features as visual dials, large numbers digital display, and pulse and temperature monitors.

Patient Security Systems of Clarendon Hills, Illinois, has developed a system for electronically monitoring wandering patients in hospital and institutions. A moisture resistant sensor, sealed in a soft foam insole and placed in the patient's shoe, provides security and comfort. The device has unlimited shelf life and requires no batteries.

Personal Emergency Response System or PERS, is a signaling device that summons help during an emergency. It's an easy to use electronic tool which can be programmed to signal a friend, relative or emergency services (police, fire department or ambulance) that help is needed. PERS provides security for older persons living alone and helps them maintain their independence. There are currently over 15 different signaling devices of this type that are available for purchase or rental.

Putting Computers to Work

New computer software which plays "matchmaker" for seniors and locations is an interesting example of technology at work. The program, called RETIRE, matches the needs, interests and means of seniors seeking a retirement location with the relevant characteristics of over four hundred cities. Nationwide Life Insurance Company, Exxon, and many other firms have purchased the software to use in their preretirement preparation programs.

Many older adults find themselves responsible for the care of elderly parents. This problem is even more acute when the elderly parent is located in another state. Because so many IBM employees are relocated to other areas around the country, the problem is one that the company felt it important enough to help solve. Using computer technology is something that comes naturally to IBM and so the giant company developed the Elder Care network, a computerized referral service which helps employees, retirees and their families locate appropriate care for elderly parents in distant cities. Work/Family Directions of Watertown, Massachusetts runs the service for IBM and other U.S. companies.

Older individuals create special challenges for designers of products and environments. The elderly tend to be smaller than the rest of the population and often lack dexterity and mobility. Advanced Living Systems, a research and development team, has developed E MANN, an electronic mannequin adaptable to most personal computers. The computerized mannequin simulates characteristics—height, reach, joint flexibility and so on—which is fed into the computer. E-Mann helps designers recreate a variety of human forms, positions and sizes and acts as an aid in their design.

The research team that developed E-Mann is a division of the Institute for Technology Development, a private, nonprofit organization based in Oxford, Mississippi. The team's goals are to identify problems encountered by older adults and to create solutions that can be used to produce real marketable products and environments. St. Catherine's Village, a new retirement development in Jackson, Mississippi, used E-Mann to design the shelves, door pulls, faucets, kitchen cabinets and other facilities in the community.

Advanced Living Systems has also launched a program for evaluating consumer products to determine their usability by older adults, and conducted extensive research with older adults to determine their perceptions of some 60 products. The research organization, currently conducting evaluation of retirement facilities, product concept analysis and mature market feasibility studies for a number of companies, is on the leading edge of mature market developments.

The trend toward self care, especially among older adults, is advanced with the recent FDA approval of a hand-held computer that enables senior diabetics to adjust their insulin dosages. The daily dosage of self-administered insulin must be adjusted regularly to accommodate changes in food consumption, stress and blood-glucose levels. While this information can be easily collected by the diabetic, translating the data into an adjusted dosage requires sophisticated mathematical calculations. Diacare System, manufactured by Healthware Corporation of Durham, North Carolina, allows the individual to feed the relevant data into the device and lets the computer do the math.

In the 1990s we will see the full blossoming of the "electronic village" concept and its impact on the older generation. This represents an opportunity for manufacturers of computer-based office at-home systems. Such systems will provide jobs for older men and women who want to work on a part-time or flexible-time basis in their own home and avoid traveling to work.

High Priority For "Low" Technology

Opening a bottle of pills or a jar of applesauce can be a frustrating experience for an older man or woman with diminished strength and lessened dexterity in the fingers. Little things like buttoning a shirt or handling the controls on an appliance can defeat a slightly arthritic but otherwise independent individual. Reduced dexterity, vision, hearing, and general mobility are among the major problems of older adults. While not in the same league as organ transplants and life-sustaining machines, "low" technology can offer simple solutions and deserve a high priority among the senior needs to be filled. Designers of packaging, apparel and appliances should be aware of the sensory and physical changes that affect the daily routine of older persons and build solutions into the product: Velcro fasteners instead of small buttons and snaps, large handled and easy-to-grip zippers, larger handles for eating utensils, levers instead of doorknobs.

Prominent among the new products that will find their way into the marketplace each year, we can expect to see a large number of products designed to correct and compensate for diminished competence. The possibilities are evident in an AARP publication entitled, *The Gadget Book: Ingenious Devices for Easier Living*. The book is a prime example of what the academicians call "low technology." It describes an array of practical items in such areas as personal care, home environment, communications, mobility, health care and recreation. The book's editor, Dennis La Buda, and other contributors spent over four years identifying some 350 devices "that would help eliminate frustration and struggle with daily activities." The products described in the book help seniors cope with the problems caused by one or a combination of factors—among them, arthritis, reduced hearing or vision, and diminished strength.

Among the 350 products in *The Gadget Book*, are assistive items such as telephone amplifiers, dialing aids, talking clocks, large-print timers, cooking and eating utensils, self-threading needles, lifts for getting to the top of the stairs, long-handled home and garden tools, and many other items. The book lists 296 manufacturers and distributors of these devices—from Atlas Surgical Belt Company of West Hollywood, Florida to Zygo Industries of Portland, Oregon—just some of the "low technology" providers that are prospering by helping mature adults maintain their independence.

Mobility, something that comes quite easily to young people, can become a major problem with advancing age. In most cases, decreased mobility is slight, but slower reaction time and physical restrictions caused by mild arthritis can create difficulties in driving or reaching for items high up, or low down, on the supermarket shelf. Merchants can help those older adults confined to wheelchairs by providing wider passageways and ramps at entrances and exits. Supermarkets can help by making shelves easier to reach. Some older persons have balance problems and are hurt badly in a fall. Easily installed grab bars in bathrooms, near the tub, shower and toilet can help prevent falls.

Designing For Seniors

In a message to Congress back in 1967, Geneva Mathiasen, then director of the National Council on Aging, said that the time had come for producers and sellers of goods to pay greater heed to the growing, and often special, needs of elderly consumers. She urged that the inventiveness of modern industrial design and engineering be utilized to create a living environment conducive to the well being of individuals as they grow older. Mathiasen believed that such products could help seniors retain their independence and perform their daily tasks with less effort and add to the enjoyment of their leisure time.

"Whether a dress has a zipper up the back or up the front may make the difference between a woman's being able to dress herself or not. The simple act of rising from a chair, or getting in and out of a taxicab, can add or subtract years to a man's apparent age, depending on how the chair or taxicab is designed." When asked to guess when automobiles would become easier to get in and out of, Ms. Mathiasen replied: "Some day maybe we'll get around to the design of automobiles once we get a good chair."

Two decades later, when London-based furniture designer Ronald Carter heard that the Hamlyn Foundation was planning a competition to encourage the commercial world "to recognize an increasingly significant market for safe, constructive products of special help to the elderly . . ." he submitted an original design for a chair. His chair, is now included with the work of 19 other winning designers in a catalogue produced by the Foundation.

Out of all of the elements of design, Carter thought that "comfort is the first priority for those whose bodies are less flexible. But this requirement can be met in ways that increase design appeal. In the line of the chair, for example. The principle of lumbar support gives you a rather beautiful form for the back legs—a very human set of curves. There is the same sort of advantage in giving the chair closed sides. They exclude draughts, conserve warmth and are visually more comfortable."

These are among the hundreds of items of daily life that can be redesigned to make life easier and more comfortable for older bodies. Most people do not fear growing old as much as they fear becoming ill and dependent. The extent to which private industry can employ technological innovation to improve the ability of mature adults to remain vital and independent is a major factor in the future of aging America.

Hartford House

One of the mature market areas showing the most public interest is in the design and construction of special housing for seniors. Hartford Insurance Company, commissioned the design of a house which would employ the latest technology and imaginative design ideas to promote safer, easier living. The Hartford House, a lifesize model with no outer walls, is touring home shows and exhibits across the country and attracting long lines of interested people wherever it appears.

The Hartford House is designed to show how the changes that people experience when they grow older "can be accommodated functionally and aesthetically in our own homes." The ideas incorporated into different areas of the Hartford house range from the inexpensive to the more costly, from the simple to the complicated. Some require professional skills, others an enthusiastic do-it-yourselfer. They may be adopted by someone building a new home, remodeling a current residence or simply making minor home improvements.

As you scan the suggestions below ask yourself, who will manufacture the products and provide the services necessary to follow all, or some, of the suggestions made by Hartford House designers?

Kitchen.   Built-in wall ovens at a height which reduces the need to bend. Because of the lessened ability of older persons to recognize odors, the dangers of an undetected gas leak are very real. They can be eliminated by an electric range or oven. Side by side refrigerator/freezers are preferable for people with limited movement. Lower wall cabinets so that they are within easy reach. Table-height work counters help people who find it difficult to stand for long periods. A flexible sink hose to fill pots on the counter or on the stovetop, eliminates the need to lift heavy pots. Toaster ovens, steam irons and other electrical appliances with automatic shut-offs avoid the possibility of fire and damage.

Bedroom. A nightlight between the bedroom and bathroom helps eliminate accidents. Smoke detectors in the bedroom can provide life saving warnings. Closets with multi-level shelving, hanging bars and hooks make contents easier to reach.

Living Room. Adaptors to metal lamps allow them to be turned on and off by touching the base, eliminating the need to grope for difficult to-turn switches. A portable security intercom, with 50 foot range, permits the resident to speak to visitors without going to the door. Furniture with strong, reliable arms and backs provide firm support. Corrected seat heights and depths make getting in and out easier.

Bathroom. A higher counter and medicine cabinet mounted at countertop level reduces back-bending and reaching. Non-slip flooring, strategically placed grab bars and hand-rails and portable benches that allow sitting while bathing prevent falling. Thermostat controls reduce high water temperatures that can burn and scald. Proper lighting is crucial for reading medicine labels or shaving.

Around the House. Levers on doors and faucets instead of knobs makes for easier handling. Large print items for bathroom scales, wall clocks, cooking timers, etc. All around lighting eliminates shadowy areas. Matte finish wallpaper and counter tops, drapery and blinds control glare and sun-light. Fire retardant material is used for draperies, upholstered furniture, mattresses, pillows, carpets, even lamp shades. A home fire extinguisher provides safety.

A large number of products are needed to follow the suggestions of Hartford House creators and designers across the country working on solutions to senior housing problems—carpets, wallcovering, window blinds, furniture, lighting, thermostats, security intercoms, flooring, stoves and ovens, refrigerators, faucets, cabinetry, smoke alarms, storage cabinets, fire extinguisher, water heat gauges, lifeline call help systems, grab bars, pill organizers. Safety seats, sink, tub and shower faucets and cabinetry, to name a few.

Among the companies whose products are featured in the Hartford House are: Armstrong World Industries, Burlington Industries, Clinitemp, Honeywell, Lazarus Contract, Lee's Carpet, Lifeline Systems, Mirro Corporation, Nora Flooring, Robert Allen Fabrics and Thomasville Furniture. These are just some of the firms that will be catering to the demands of the mature market in the 1990s and well into the 21st century.

Find The Need And Fill It

Technology helped create the phenomenon of an aging America, and industry is positioned to reap the rewards of its creation. For companies large and small, from large international corporations to shoestring entrepreneurs, the key to success in winning a large share of the mature market remains "find the need and fill it."

Here are some of the needs of older Americans (i.e., opportunities for industry), now and in the months and years ahead . . .

Food and Beverages.   In food products, the need continues for more high nutrition, low fat, low salt and low cholesterol meals and snacks and smaller portion packaging; in beverages, less sugary soft drinks and more natural bottled water (carbonated and non-carbonated) with light flavoring, light beer and light alcoholic drinks.

Home Security.   There is a rising demand from older adults for security devices and closed-circuit TV security systems, fire alarms and special telephones for emergency help.

Packaging.   Packaging can be improved to satisfy the needs of seniors by better labeling, larger type for prices and ingredients, more visible contents, and more convenience in handling, carrying and storing.

Delivery Services. Because seniors don't always have adequate transportation or the ability to carry heavy loads, delivery services for restaurant food, groceries, drugs, dry cleaning, books and video tapes will provide an important service.

Apparel. Apparel manufacturers and retailers should be aware of the special needs of older adults for more comfortable, appropriately sized clothing with easy to use zippers and velcro closures. (Note: Comfortable doesn't mean dowdy or unfashionable.)

Housing. To accommodate possible physical limitations of older residents, new homes and modifications to existing homes should include lower shelves, larger access ways, safety rails and grab bars, better lighting, etc.

Financial Services. Special banking services, conservative investment and insurance vehicles and estate planning are among the major areas of financial services needs for seniors.

Preventive Medicine and Fitness. New methods of preventive medicine and devices for monitoring health, exercise equipment designed specifically for older adults, exercise and fitness programs and lectures and mutual help networks can help seniors keep healthy and help check the soaring cost of medical care.

Education. Programs are needed to teach new skill for avocational activities and second careers. Also, special college-level courses for older students and the employment of mature teachers with life experience.

Culture and Self-Fulfillment. Among the items in this category are large-print books and magazines, lectures, arts and crafts programs, etc.

Recreation. Home entertainment, tapes and games specifically for seniors. Golf and fishing equipment and gardening paraphernalia designed for mature adults.

Travel. Special travel packages and cruises for seniors. Discount programs for transportation and hotels.

Seniors Relate to New Technologies

You can't teach an old dog new tricks? Don't you believe it. The assumption that older people are not interested and closed to the advantages of technology is a fallacy. Study after study reveals that older men and women are open to new technologies where the perceived benefit is meaningful. They are using calculators and personal computers, working the Automatic Teller Machines (ATMs) at money stations in metropolitan areas, keeping their audio equipment, VCRS and microwave ovens cooking and patronizing scanner equipped supermarkets in their neighborhood.

The Markle Foundation study on aging in America investigated the relationship between seniors and technology. The study finds that seniors use technology to enhance, not to replace, activity:

"Indeed, there seems to be a mis-match between the nature of many of today's new consumer technologies—designed for convenience and saving time—and the needs of retired Americans, which are more clearly related to lifestyle enhancement:

- Not to save time, but to make it more meaningful.

- Not to replace doing a chore, but only to lighten it.

- Not to minimize social contact, but to facilitate it.

- Not to avoid getting out, but to encourage it."

An indication of how well seniors are able to adapt to our high tech world is apparent in research at the University of Georgia. The University used a computer as a model to analyze the memory retention of older adults. According to researcher Dr. Denise Park, participants in the research were very positive about computer use and had no phobias or hesitancy about their use. She notes that while some participants had slightly slower reaction times than younger persons, when allowed to learn at their own pace, older adults were able to cope with the complexities of high tech equipment. Other research at Georgia Tech on word processing software, showed that seniors do not lack the ability or desire to conquer computers.

Researchers offer software and hardware manufacturers some design suggestions to help seniors working on computers . . .

- Because some seniors have impaired vision, avoid green and blue screens which make characters more difficult to distinguish. Amber colored screens are preferable.

- The size of the characters on the monitor should be larger. (Apply MacIntosh MacWrite word processing and Vista System made by Telesensory Systems for IBM compatible personal computers provide large type on the monitors.)

- Programs that use "mouse" equipment require a high degree of manual dexterity. Adjustment in this equipment to allow less precision would help older computer-users.

SeniorNet

If anyone needs proof of the way that older adults are taking to high technology consider SeniorNet, an organization which operates an "international community of computer using seniors." The organization provides on-line computer network services to individual members and to local sites in the U.S. and Canada where computers are available for use by seniors. In addition to operating an on-line network, SeniorNet organizes annual conferences and conducts research on the use of computers by older adults.

The computer-linked network allows men and women, 55 years of age and over, to communicate on a wide range of subjects. It can be thought of as an "electronic city of seniors" who communicate and participate in activities that are "only as far away as one's fingertips on a keyboard." Members send and receive electronic messages, and may participate in forum discussions on health and fitness, retirement planning, or political issues. They can also make travel arrangements, check stock quotations or contribute ideas to the on-line archives.

Dr. Mary Furlong of the University of San Francisco is the founder and Executive Director of SeniorNet, which she reports has two thousand seniors currently "on line," with the number growing at an accelerated rate as the idea spreads and more sites are opened.

The project depends on business and professional organizations to support local computer-equipped sites which are a key element of the program. Such sites are now operating in locations from New York to California and Hawaii, and from Florida to Washington State and Alberta, Canada. One of the most active of the new sites is sponsored by Stahl Eye Associates in Garden City, Long Island, just outside of New York City. Dr. Norman Stahl, the head of the sponsoring company, sees SeniorNet as a way to show his company's interest in the community. A natural tie-in with eye care, many other computer-equipped Senior-Net sites are being underwritten by ophthalmologists and eye care centers.

Among the leading companies and organizations that help support the project are Apple Computer, Pacific Telesis, Bank of America, U.S. West, Pacific Bell, the Out-Patient Ophthalmic Surgery Society and the Markle Foundation.

The ability of seniors to relate to new technology is confirmed by the work of Dr. Margaret Wylde, at the Advanced Living Systems Division of the Institute for Technology Development. Dr. Wylde studied a group of women 57 to 75 years of age to determine their ability to use technology. She concluded that seniors are not necessarily wary of high tech, even of an interactive video system that included a computer, a laser video disk player and a high resolution monitor. The staff examiner provided no instruction to the group other than designating one subject to control the program by touching the screen.

"My findings with this group of senior adults goes against the stereotype," Dr. Wylde said. She found that even though participants had little experience with basic technology, 94 percent of the participants found the interactive system easier to use and better than a presentation by a speaker. None was intimidated by the equipment, and more than 80 percent found it an effective way to present complex information. Researchers at the Institute reported that seniors prefer high technology when there is a clear benefit.

PART THREE
THE PRODUCTS

"Someday when I'm tired and gray, I hope I'm like today's McDonald's—way too old to be looking so good. I know they'll follow my age group to the end. One day I'll shuffle in, and there will be on the menu: 'McOatmeal.'"

Penny Moser, in an article in Fortune magazine on marketing leadership of fast-food giant McDonald's

CHAPTER SIX

FOOD AND BEVERAGES

Food packagers and supermarket buyers are keenly aware of who buys what and are moving quickly to give their customers what they want. They know that . . .

- Americans 55 and over purchased 46 percent of all decaffeinated coffee, 32 percent of all margarine, 37 percent of all over-the counter drugs, 28 percent of canned soup products, 30 percent of all instant coffee and 30 percent of all food consumed at home. ("The 55+ Market," Jordan, Case & McGrath Inc., New York, N.Y.)

- Older shoppers are major buyers of food products low in cholesterol (such as fish, turkey and chicken). They purchase most of the products featuring low salt, low calorie, and high calcium; they prefer frozen foods, microwavable foods, and packaged foods with smaller sized portions. (Progressive Grocer, Aug '86)

- Seventy-two percent of people age 65 and over say that nutrition is a primary concern, as opposed to the 19-24 group where there is the least nutritional interest. (Food Marketing Institute, 1988 Study.)

The changes made in soft drink products exemplify the way that industry is accommodating older tastes. The sugar and caffeine-laden Cola drinks that are so popular with teenagers, lose their appeal with age. In response to changing adults tastes, a new wave of adult beverages with natural ingredients and no preservatives gained favor with an aging population. In 1987, these "softer" soft drinks rang up more than $1.9 billion in sales, and captured 5.1 percent of the soft drink market. Carbonated water, flavored seltzer and other light drinks popular with older adults are racking up sales in restaurants and supermarkets across the country.

The frozen food industry is also altering the content of its products to appeal to the diets and palates of older consumers. The reputation of frozen food products as being loaded with the big three prohibitions of the mature diet—fat, sodium and cholesterol—has stopped many an older hand from reaching for the latest frozen meal on the supermarket shelf. ConAgra, a huge food company with annual sales of $10 billion, and second only to the Campbell Soup Company in the frozen-dinner market, is trying to change all that and capitalize on the diet-conscious demands of older food shoppers. It has come out with "Healthy Choice," a new line of quick preparation entrees which the company says are the first frozen prepared-meals to meet the heart association's dietary guidelines.

The new line was inspired by Charles M. Harper, the company's 61 year old chairman, who craved the tasty food that he was no longer allowed because of a heart attack. Early attempts by ConAgra's kitchens to create frozen meals without the forbidden ingredients failed to produce a product that met taste tests, but the company finally hit upon a mix of flavorings which gives the Healthy Choice line its tastiness and compensates for the absence of fat, sodium and ingredients containing cholesterol. Food products which are nutritious *and* tasty will find a huge market in the senior population.

A study of consumer use of various grocery products, that tested readers of *Modern Maturity* magazine (median age of group studied, 67.4), confirms the substantial consumption of certain food and beverages by older men and women. In the listing that follows, the first number after the product category shows the percent of the older households that use the product; the second figure shows the average of packages, cans, or jars that the respondent used in the last *30 days.*

Canned or Jarred Vegetables, 59.5% / 8.5
Canned or Jarred Fruit, 54% / 5.3
Flavored Gelatin Dessert, 45.6% / 3.9
Regular Yogurt, 27.2 / 6.7
Frozen Main Courses, 25.2 / 6.7

In these heavily used products, the first number after the product shows the percent of the older households that use the product; the second figure shows the average of packages, cans or jars used in the last 7 *days.*

Cold Breakfast Cereals, 76.3% / 2.8
Hot Breakfast Cereals, 43.4% / 2.4
Natural Cheese, 65.1% / 1.8
Canned Soup, 64.6% / 2.5
Cottage Cheese, 58.9% / 1.6

Of the *Modern Maturity* readers surveyed, 67.1 percent purchased special "diet type" foods in the last 30 days. These included caffein-free beverages, additive and preservative-free items and foods low in sugar, sodium, cholesterol and calories. More than 60% of older adults drank one or more types of alcoholic beverages including Bourbon and Scotch Whiskey, Vodka, Gin and Rum, Brandy and Cognac. Close to 25 percent drank domestic table wine and 7 percent drank imported wine. Beer consumption is light among seniors: 16 percent drank regular beer, 13 percent drank light beer and 5 percent drank imported beer.

Packaging

Since seniors represent such a large part of the market for foods and other packaged items, the packaging of such products becomes an important factor in their marketing. Herbert Mayers, a New York Design and marketing consultant, told *Mature Market* that "packaging must accommodate the special needs and limitation of older adults, especially those elderly with declining visual and motor capabilities."

Many seniors have problems in their ability to focus, resolve images, distinguish among colors and adapt to different lighting conditions. In order to create packages designed to attract older shoppers making their way down the supermarket aisle, Mayers suggested more color contrast, "the greater the contrast between two colors, or between an image and its background, the easier it is to see."

Reds, oranges and yellows cause few color perception problems for older eyes, but many seniors have difficulty discerning among blues, greens and violets. And, since consumers of all age have difficulty with colors too similar to the background colors, color values must be carefully chosen for legibility.

Crowded shelves, at supermarkets and mass merchandise general stores, make it important that package designers address the difficulty older consumers have to find what they're looking for or to notice new items on the shelf. Small figures and type under 12 points in size are difficult for older eyes; script and baroque type-styles create clutter. Ample spacing between lines helps readability. Also, keep copy on packages to a minimum and break it down into small, readable units. When possible, keep the design clean and simple.

It's important to keep in mind that older people are careful shoppers. They tend to read labels and look for information about ingredients, nutritional values, expiration dates and instructions for preparation. Mature consumers are brand loyal; when creating new designs for packages it's advisable, to provide continuity by carrying over components from previous package designs.

The bold display, of features that are important to older men and women, is crucial. When appropriate such features as "Low Salt," "No Salt Added," "Low Cholesterol" and "Low Far Content" should be displayed, loud and clear, on the package. Here are some of the characteristics of good packaging designed to capture the attention of mature consumers:

- Strong brand identification.
- Clear, legible product description.
- Bright contrasting colors appropriate to the product.
- Large, no-nonsense type styling.
- Secondary copy on features important to seniors.
- Use of color to differentiate variations of the same basic product.
- Communication of price and value.

Competitive items on the supermarket shelf are screaming for attention. Creative package design, that addresses the special interests, needs and visual limitations of mature consumers, can determine a product's popularity.

Supermarket Shopping

Consider the one retail establishment that plays a key role in the life of today's seniors—the supermarket, provider of sustenance. In general, older men and women have a positive attitude toward supermarket shopping. They appreciate the convenience of having a store where they can obtain their favorite foods and most of their household needs. They praise supermarkets for the wide variety of products carried and they like the exposure to new products that supermarkets provide. They also like the idea of mingling with younger persons at supermarkets. These are some of the findings of a study by The Food Marketing Institute, whose 1,100 food wholesale and retail members represent half of all the grocery stores in the United States.

The study also documents some of the problems that elderly consumers have with supermarket shopping. According to the study, "The physical problems they encounter when shopping serve as an unpleasant reminder;

but so do some remedies to their shopping difficulties that single them out for special treatment. For instance, some of the panalists rejected measures such as special shopping hours or discount coupons for the elderly even though such programs would help alleviate serious problems."

A number of suggestions emerged from the study:

- Offer more products that meet the dietary needs of older persons—products with reduced levels of salt and sugar.

- Find ways to help older shoppers locate special diet foods—color coded shelf tags, for example.

- Use larger and bolder print on product labels.

- Package foods in smaller quantities suitable for smaller households.

- Redesign boxes, jars and bottles so that they are easier for consumers with less dexterity or strength to open them.

- Install a buzzer, phone or intercom in the aisles so that customers can ask questions or seek help.

- Stock merchandise so that items popular with older customers are easily accessible without bending or reaching.

- Smaller, easier to maneuver shopping carts would make shopping easier.

Somebody's paying attention. The February 1988 newsletter of the Food Marketing Institute listed some recent changes that supermarkets are making to accommodate older customers:

- Benches and restrooms "have appeared where there were none."

- Bus and transportation arrangements are being installed.

- Motorized shopping carts and blood-pressure testing machines are available in a growing number of supermarkets.

- New special services and discounts are offered to seniors.

- Employee training programs now include instruction on assisting older shoppers.

The food store industry's newsletter commented on the distinct shopping patterns and product preferences of older shoppers: "They are more likely to be found shopping in the morning hours, spend a little less than other age groups and look for smaller packages." This point is confirmed by Jim Thompson, manager of consumer affairs for the AARP. He says that seniors care about single-item packaging because "their household size is smaller."

The findings of an AARP study provide other clues to senior preferences: Older consumers don't mind buying high-ticket, high margin items. They are more concerned with product attributes and services than they are with price. They appreciate helpful personnel and baggers at the checkout counter and enjoy the social interaction of the shopping experience. They tend to shop more frequently than other groups and like to take their time when they do shop. For many seniors, a trip to the supermarket is the big outing of their day.

Supermarket Roundup

Some of the senior programs conducted by supermarket chains are listed in the Food Industry's newsletter. They provide ideas applicable to other retail businesses interested in providing a community service for seniors while at the same time courting their loyal patronage.

Membership Cards Randalls Food Markets in Houston, Texas issued silver courtesy cards to their customers 60 and over. The card makes them eligible for free coffee, blood pressure checkups, free check cashing and a 10 percent discount on prescriptions filled at the store. Every Tuesday is "Senior's Day" at Randalls. A special $1.99 meal is served and seniors receive discount coupons good throughout that week.

Volunteer Programs   King Soopers in Denver, Colorado conducts a "Shop for a Friend" program where employees who volunteer are matched with homebound or elderly seniors who cannot shop on their own. Says program spokesman Steve Katzenberger, "It's like a permanent adoption. We have 320 employees in 67 stores serving the needs of 325 shut-ins. It almost works out on a one-to-one basis—one person gets to know a senior or handicapped person and develops a friendship." The store won a Presidential Citation for community service from President Reagan for their "Shop for a Friend" program.

Rest Areas   Publix Super Markets in Florida accommodates its clientele of retired seniors by providing benches and chairs for resting. They have a training film for employees on how to treat older customers. (In a reader's survey by *Golden Years* magazine, employee courtesy was one of the major reasons given by customers on why they shopped at Publix.)

Free Information   Giant Foods in Maryland distributes an average of 13,000 free, *Shopping Sense for Seniors* booklets in its 146 supermarkets in the Virginia-Maryland-D.C. area. The food chain also sponsors Tel Med Health Information, a call-in service with more than 250 tape recorded mesages on health and medical problems.

Free Transportation   Stew Leonards in Danbury, Connecticut, has two Greyhound buses that go to 30 senior citizen homes seven days a week to pick up shoppers and return them to their homes. The supermarket chain makes a point of hiring retired people and considers them a tremendous asset to its business.

Older consumers are more likely to choose a super-market for its convenient location than are younger consumers, but price is also a factor for seniors as it is for other age groups. A study by Johnson & Johnson Products of 11,000 consumers found that more younger shoppers than seniors chose to patronize a store on the basis of price, while more seniors than younger shoppers chose a store because of location. More seniors than younger shoppers considered service an important factor in their store selection.

According to Fred R. Patterson, Johnson & Johnson's manager of home health care marketing, Americans over 55 tend to favor national brands and appreciate personal service. He says that "There is a great need for us to concentrate on training our employes in sensitivity to the elderly.

A Retailer's Guide to Unmet Needs

How well are retailers doing in satisfying the needs of older consumers? To find answers to this question, Zarrel Lambert, Professor of Marketing at Auburn University in Auburn, Alabama, conducted a survey of individuals in two age groups, 55 to 64 and 65 and older. The survey found that older consumers had the following concerns and preferences:

Discounts 59 percent of the 55 to 64 group and 53 percent of those 65 and over called for senior citizen discounts and wanted them applied to a wider variety of products and services. A number of respondents to the Auburn University survey wanted discounts increased above the customary 10 percent.

Customer-Personnel Relationships About 20 percent of the 55 to 64 group and 25 percent of those over 65 wanted better treatment from store personnel. They wanted older consumers to be treated with more courtesy, dignity and patience. Comments indicated that older consumers were unhappy with the disinterest, impatience and rudeness they perceived in store employees.

Locating Products   Approximately 19 percent of both groups complained about their difficulty in finding what they were looking for and some requested personal assistance in finding products instead of having to "flounder around."

Hard to Read Price Tags and Labels   About 10 percent of both groups complained about small blurred print on tags and labels.

Checkout Counter Service   Some participants in the survey felt that faster checkout services should be provided so older consumers could avoid standing in long lines.

Package Sizes   Older consumers have smaller appetites and fewer people in the household. Large packages of food often spoil or become stale before the food is consumed. (Retailers can influence food processors to offer the option of smaller packages.)

Rest Facilities and Rest Rooms   Shopping can wear out older men and women. Benches and chairs are inexpensive items that would be appreciated and increase the shoppers "staying power." Clean, comfortable rest rooms are an important convenience for mature shoppers.

Other concerns mentioned in the Auburn study include inconvenient parking, the lack of assistance in carrying out packages and narrow, crowded aisles. Some suggested that stores designate certain hours for elderly shoppers, an idea that has been tried with questionable success: many seniors resent being isolated as a group and shopping only with other seniors.

The concerns and preferences of those surveyed may best be summed-up in one respondent's comment sited in *MSU Business Topics*: "I would pay a little more to shop in a store that went after the business of retirement-age people."

Restaurants

"Seniors are a big part of our reason for being," says Joseph Harrera, marketing director for Denny's restaurant chain. Adults 55 and over make up almost one-third of the customers in their 1,200 restaurants across the nation. The restaurant chain recently placed ads in *Modern Maturity* and *50 Plus* magazines to advertise its new senior menu—13 different menu items which feature smaller portions, lower fat, salt and cholesterol, and prices that are 10 to 25 percent lower than standard items on the menu. The dishes are approved by the American Heart Association.

Focus groups in areas with large senior populations in Florida and Arizona revealed that older men and women worry about their health and about restaurant prices but they still want a selection when they're eating out. Herrara credits the advertising to announce the new menu with an eight percent jump in senior business. Advertising is just part of Denny's marketing efforts in attracting seniors. The restaurant chain promotes itself through public relations and community activities which include participation in senior conventions and sponsorship of "senior days" at local fairs. At the fairs, Denny's staff distribute discount coupons and hold raffles for a year's worth of free dinners.

The 55 to 64 segment of the population dines out an average of three times a week. For people over age 65, eating out at restaurants drops to an average of 1.8 meals a week. While both of these figures fall slightly below the total average of 3.7 meals per week for the general population, the National Restaurant Association's 1986 Meal Consumption Behavior Study, showed an increase in spending by older adults for meals and snacks away from home. Since 1978, eating out has increased by 6 percent overall, but it has increased by 21 percent among people 50 and over. Mature diners are patronizing fast food restaurants and cafeterias substantially more than they did a decade ago. In fact, an association study in 1986 showed that more than 40 percent of the mature groups' restaurant meals were at moderately priced, family-style restaurants.

The study also showed that . . .

- Seniors 65 and over are more likely than younger people to patronize expensive, upscale restaurants.

- While they don't have the same enthusiasm as younger age groups for new restaurant concepts, seniors frequent restaurants offering specialty foods such as barbecued food, pasta, gourmet burgers and Asian fast food.

- Four out of ten restaurant visits by mature consumers were to fast food restaurants.

- The specialty restaurants most heavily patronized by seniors offer bakery items, hot dogs, and premium ice cream.

Seniors prefer to eat at familiar restaurants that offer pleasant, dignified surroundings and a sense of well-being. They're less impressed by fad dishes and more conscious of the quality of the food. Anything less than good quality food and courteous service, will turn away seniors. And since restaurants are a popular subject of conversation, it will turn away their friends just as quickly.

A pleasant, quiet atmosphere, comfortable seating, and cleanliness are among the features that seniors appreciate most in a restaurant. To older adults, eating out is a social experience, and contact with their peers and restaurant personnel is an important consideration. Single seniors, like younger singles, are particularly interested in the social aspects of dining out.

Even though older Americans represent a great potential for increasing restaurant business, other than Denny's and a few other mid-scale family restaurants, the industry has neglected to make the kind of changes in their menus, pricing and service that will attract this large and well-to-do group. For example, increasing the number of seafood items on the menu can help attract senior patronage Older restaurant customers are more than twice as likely to order seafood as those adults 18 to 49. In addition, knowing that seniors are less likely to want an extensive menu or wine list and that they are less than half as likely as their younger counterparts to purchase take-out food can help the restaurant that caters to this market to cut costs by eliminating those features that are not important to seniors.

Restauranteurs interested in building their base of older customers, will find that salad bars are a popular attraction. According to Vance Research Services of Lincolnshire, Illinois, food bars are more popular with the older generation than with the young; over 16 percent of the 50-59 group frequent a salad bar two or more times a week. The 50 to 59 group was the top patron of salad bars, with the 60 and over restaurant patrons right behind.

Diet and nutrition is increasingly important to seniors. Three quarters of the males between 45 and 54 surveyed in a National Restaurant Association study, said they restricted their intake of cholesterol and fat. Eighty-one percent consumed fiber and 61 percent controlled their use of salt. Of the females surveyed, 90 percent said they restricted salt in their diets, and 70 percent controlled their intake of fat and cholesterol.

Although seniors may not be receptive to all health-foods, especially non-traditional restaurant food, diet and nutrition are major selling points in attracting older adults. One of the best ways that a restaurant can build its base of mature customers is by allowing special diet requests, such as cooking without salt, or substituting unsaturated fat corn oil for butter when sauteing. By indicating on the menu that such special requests will be honored, the restaurant can become a favorite eating place among older adults.

CHAPTER SEVEN
ON THE MOVE

Free time and disposable income (and the physical stamina to enjoy them) make many of today's seniors ideal candidates for a variety of products and services not always associated with the mature market. In this chapter we will see where these more active lifestyles have created corresponding needs in the marketplace. If, after all, today's seniors are on the move, its only logical that they'll need places and ways to go, and something to do and wear when they get there.

Sports and Fitness

"Unless we begin to realize that there are more pairs of Adidas than orthopedic shoes in the elderly's closet, we will continue to serve the stereotope, not the actuality."—John K. Grace, vice president of Gray Advertising.

Earlier in this century, medical advise favored rest and moderate physical activity for older persons. Not any longer. Increasingly, doctors have come to recognize the enormous mental and physical health benefits in exercise and sports. The resulting increase of physical activity has contributed to the dramatic gains in life expectancy and the sense of well-being that has enriched the lives of millions of people. In order to look better and feel better, they have latched on to the exercise and fitness craze—with a vengeance.

As might be expected, walking is the most popular form of exercise among older Americans. According to a study by the National Sporting Goods Association (NSGA), among adults, 55 years of age and older, almost 16 million (or roughly 31 percent of Americans in that age segment) walked for exercise.

Seniors also participate in a great many sports not usually associated with the later years. According to the NSGA, the number and percent of the 55+ population participating in the ten most popular sports activities are as follows:

	Participants (in millions)	As a percent of Participants in Sport
Exercise Walking	15.9	27.4 percent
Fishing	6.7	14.6
Swimming	6.2	9.4
Bowling	6.2	15.4
Boating (Motor)	5.5	17.8
Bicycle Riding	4.9	9.2
Camping	4.5	10.2
Exercise with Equipment	3.8	11.0
Golf	3.6	17.8
Billiards	2.8	9.6

Marketers looking at this list hear the cash register ringing from the hundreds of millions of dollars spent each year for walking shoes, fishing gear, swimming apparel, bowling balls, motor boats, bicycles, camping equipment, health club memberships, exercise equipment, golf clubs, golf carts, billiard cues and billiard tables. Not to mention the equipment and other paraphernalia needed to participate in numerous other activities such as aerobics, tennis, raquetball, jogging and skiing.

As with marketing exercise equipment for other age segments, it's important to remember the differences in interests between the sexes. Thomas B. Doyle, NSGA Director of Information and Research, reports that "Although exercise walking was the most popular activity among men and women 55 year or older, twice as many women as men are exercise walkers. There are also distinct differences in other interests among men and women in this age group. Fishing was the second most popular activity with men with 4.5 million participants while bowling was the second most popular activity among women in this age group, with 3.7 million participants."

In total, more than 6.2 million adults over the age 55 bowl, at least once a year, at one of the 8,000 bowling centers across the country. A survey by the National Bowling Council reveals that over one-half in that age group went bowling more than 15 times during the year. The sport has a great deal going for it among older Americans; bowling facilities are usually convenient and close to home, it's inexpensive and can be played in any weather. Older bowlers say it's a good way to make new friends and many belong to Senior Bowling Leagues.

Travel

Seniors 50 and over travel farther and travel for longer periods of time than their younger counterparts. They are traveling by every possible mode. For the most part, they are experienced travelers with varied interests.

Almost every day of the year, you'll find older Americans walking the Great Wall of China, cruising in the Mediterranean, riding the rapids of the Colorado River or taking a short holiday at a hotel less than a hundred miles from home. In any case, they're on the move. They have the time, the money and the desire to get around and enjoy new places and new experiences.

Consequently, the mature traveler is the mainstay of many travel-industry suppliers—the car rentals, airlines, cruiselines, bus companies and railroads that get them there; the hotels, resorts and restaurants that shelter and feed them, the travel agents that put it all together; and the hundreds of other types of businesses that depend on travelers, vacationers and tourists for their livelihoods. Still, most travel industry leaders believe that the mature market has not been fully penetrated and that greater accommodation to the needs and desires of the older traveler will bring vast numbers of new customers into the market.

There are patterns, in the travel and vacation behavior of seniors, that serve as guidelines for travel industry suppliers. According to Margaret Amein, research analyst at the U.S. Travel Data Center, seniors 55 and over, comprise 23 percent of all travelers and 63 percent of those who travel do so for vacation. She reports that seniors average longer overnight stays than the rest of the population, that seniors tend to travel with just one other individual, that 5 percent use package-inclusive tours and 12 percent consult a travel agent and have their trip booked by a travel agent.

The Mature Market Report estimates that seniors spend $51 million a year on travel—a figure expected to grow to $56 million by 1995 and climb to $65 million by 2030. Other findings show that seniors represent 60 percent of all cruise travelers, 57 percent of all golfing vacationers and 44 percent of all adult passports issued.

Data compiled for the National Geromarket Omnibus Study by Goldring and Company, a Chicago-based research firm, reinforces the new image of the energetic, active mature traveler. More than 90 percent of the 2,600 seniors, surveyed nationwide, took at least one vacation trip in North America during the last five years. The same high percentage plans at least one trip during the next three years, with a large portion planning at least two or more trips. More than 70 percent will vacation by car; more than 50 percent plan a flying vacation within three years; 15 percent will travel by bus; 9 percent by camper or RV; and 8 percent will take a train during their holiday.

Of the same number surveyed, more than 30 percent went overseas during the last five years and more than 43 percent plan an overseas trip within three years. While cruise ship vacations seem a natural for seniors, only 17 percent cruised in the last five years, but 28 percent plan to do so within the next three years.

As expected, the mature travel more for pleasure and less for business than the younger adult. In 1984, the 50+

domestic traveler accounted for 30 percent of all estimated travel, 30 percent of all air trips, 32 percent of hotel and motel nights and 72 percent of all Recreational Vehicle travel. Travelers over 50 are more likely to travel for entertainment such as sightseeing, theatre, historic sites and shopping junkets. Outdoor recreation is not a high travel priority with seniors.

In regard to international travel, in 1983 the older traveler accounted for nearly 44 percent of all adult passports issued and 34 percent of all all-inclusive package tours. According to government figures for that year, there was a 9 percent increase in passports issued to all age groups, but a 16 percent increase in passports issued to individuals 50 and over. Of almost all the overseas trips reported by those over 55, almost 50 percent went to Western Europe, compared with 39 percent of all age groups. The 55+ age group represents 37 percent of all travelers to Eastern Europe, 34 percent of travelers to Africa, 30 percent to Western Europe, 20 percent to the Far East and Central America and 16 percent of travelers to the Caribbean.

To promote business with the senior set, and to help fill empty seats on their planes, some airlines are promoting plans that allow older travelers to purchase one year's worth of airplane travel for a single payment at a highly favorable price. One such program, the "Get-Up-and-Go Passport," offers "virtually unlimited travel" on Continental Airlines and Eastern Airlines to 127 domestic destinations in the U.S., Canada, Puerto Rico and the Virgin Islands. Additional destinations are available for a nominal "add-on" fee. Plans are underway at other airlines to offer similar single-payment annual programs to seniors traveling for pleasure.

AARP director Robert Forbes believes that health, finances and education are the factors that most affect senior travel. He see a trend among seniors for less packaged tours and, "as long as people have their health and can afford it they will more likely opt for independent travel." He also sees a trend among seniors toward shorter, more frequent vacations.

A matter of concern to the older traveler is the penalty for cancellation. Because seniors are more decisive in their planning and rarely change travel plans impulsively, they resent paying cancellation penalties, especially in circumstances due to health problems. It makes sense, therefore, that travel suppliers recommend or include insurance to cover cancellation, as well as such "peace of mind" insurance as baggage, medical transportation and health care abroad. Addressing these areas of concern to seniors can attract new customers and keep present customers happy.

Transportation

Most older Americans prefer to rely on the automobile, driving themselves or relying on the driving of friends and relatives to transport them back and forth from work, shopping, visiting friends, senior centers and recreational facilities. Walking, by preference or necessity, is also an important mode of transportation for seniors. In fact, more seniors walk, for recreation and to get from here to there, than do the young and middle-aged.

Large numbers of seniors continue to drive well into their later years, and the automobile continues to be an important means of local transportation and for extended vacation trips during their early retirement years. Only when they are well into old age does transportation become a problem. Aside from having a car available, the elderly are concerned about losing their license, because of physical or visual impairment, or being denied auto insurance for similar reasons.

For non-drivers who do not live in areas where public mass-transportation is available, special bus systems and taxis are just about the only way to get around. When affordable, taxis, with their personalized, private, door to door service, are preferred. Taxi systems that make regular runs to popular destinations and provide share-a-ride plans for seniors may be a more reasonable alternative to running a bus for few travelers. Since older persons tend to travel during off-peak periods, it makes sense to have reduced taxi-rates for seniors traveling during off hours when the taxis would otherwise be idle. Both the consumers and the taxi systems could benefit from such an arrangement.

Due to changing demographics, and the decline in elementary and high school registrations, school buses are standing idle in many communities. Some of those communities are putting these buses back into commission providing transportation for seniors. Transportation services provided by retailers, hospitals and medical facilities are also helping to fill the need.

Retail Shopping

Older consumers have a special relationship with retail stores, large and small. The corner druggist confirms the doctor's choice of medicine and helps explain the dosage. The hardware clerk advises on the size of the screw while he's making up a new set of keys. Shopping at famous department stores, like Marshall Field's in Chicago, is a family tradition—"My grandmother shopped here, so did my mother. I would feel disloyal if I went anywhere else for a Christmas gift for my granddaughter." Very ofter, the name of the retailer is like a second label on the product, it reinforces the brand and comforts the consumer.

A report, sponsored by the Andrus Foundation, on retail shopping behavior of persons 60 and over, indicated that older shoppers are more concerned than younger people with the personal interaction aspect of their shopping experience. Although older people perceive themselves as conformist shoppers (as opposed to innovators or option leaders in shopping, fashion and general behavior contexts), they are nevertheless, self-confident shoppers. The findings of the study also suggest that the older person prefers a more limited range of items and variety of merchandise in a store. Specialty stores and special departments in larger stores would be ideally suited to accommodating the preferences of older shoppers.

Many of the nation's leading retailers have special programs designed to court older consumers and reinforce that special relationship so important to that age group. Sears Roebuck & Co., created the Mature Outlook Club, which, for a $7.50 annual membership fee, provides customers with a variety of discounts on many products and services. There is, of course, nothing new about offering older customers discounts. What is new is the retailer's attitude as expressed by Bill Strauss, executive director of Sear's Mature Outlook, "Before you gave discounts because the elderly couldn't afford things. Now, it is entirely different. The new programs are being offered because they [the mature market] represent a major opportunity market."

K-Mart, the nation's second largest retailer after Sears, set aside special hours on a December Saturday morning for a "senior citizen shopping spree." In addition to refreshments and placing chairs in the aisles, customers received free gift wrapping, mailing services and other "extras."

Hecht's Department Stores, which are owned by May Department Stores, has created OASIS (the Older Adult Service and Information System), an ambitious program of educational, cultural and "wellness" activities for its older customers. There are 20 OASIS Centers permanently assigned space in stores in 15 cities. OASIS has 77,000 members whose average age is 65; although predominantly female, the membership includes many couples as well.

OASIS was originally funded with a grant from the U.S. Department of Health and Human Services' Administration on Aging, and subsequently supported by The May Foundation and local social agencies. The OASIS program is often held up as a model of government-business partnership and what can be accomplished when these two forces cooperate. "I don't know of any other arrangement like it in the county," says Joe Puhalia, president of the Prince George Private Industry Council, a private, non-profit organization in Maryland. "I think it's an excellent partnership, and it would be good to see more like it. The network of communication between business and the government benefits the people they are trying to serve—in this case, the senior citizens."

While the store management does not view OASIS as a marketing tool to attract seniors, it has certainly had that effect. As quoted in the *Washington Post*, a 66 year old member of an OASIS exercise class said, "I'll invariably leave a half hour early and shop here. It's a real opportunity to shop."

Marylen Mann, the founder and director of OASIS, says that the program was initiated after a study showed that older adults preferred activities at shopping centers and other urban locations, including schools and senior citizen centers. She says that even though people were bored and lonely and wanted programs, they didn't want to take part in programs at senior citizen centers because they were intimidating, and "the department store was regarded as neutral territory. The people felt they were not going to a place for the elderly, but rather to one of the most active places in the American scene."

Fashion and Apparel

At a fashion show, Britain's Prime Minister Margaret Thatcher, who was 64 in 1989, was shown a black wool, bare shouldered, pants suit by Anne Klein. "It's lovely," she said, "but it's not for me or a woman of my age."

The Prime Minister has excellent taste and a finely tuned sense of what is appropriate at her age and in her position. That mix of attractive, fashionable and "appropriate" can serve as a guide for apparel manufacturers designing for the mature woman.

When sales of womens' sportwear started to decline, manufacturers and retailers looked for reasons. Joseph Ellis, a Goldman Sachs security analyst who follows the fashion industry, believes that the industry is ignoring older women and making clothes for women in their teens and early twenties, even though that market segment is shrinking.

Retailers observe that shopping is no fun for aging Baby Boomers and older women. Most of the clothes on the racks look too young for them and don't fit right because they're cut for more youthful, flat-bellied figures. Mr. Ellis says that while most retailers are searching for the next hot item, the older customer is saying "Forget hot—give me something that is stylish, flattering and fits.'"

The fashion industry needs to be reminded that men and women don't suddenly lose their interest in fashionable clothes and accessories after their 50th birthday. They are looking for clothes that are fashionable but not outlandish—clothes that are appropriate to their age, local styles and self image.

The recognition of behavioral differences among older clothing shoppers is an important first step in courting the mature market. Once the decision is made to target the older adults an effective marketing mix of production, distribution, and promotion must be made.

Levi Strauss's "Action Slacks" for men and "Bend Over" slacks for women are examples of fashionable products made with the older shopper in mind. A study by Marx and Newman Company, distributors of Liz Claiborne shoes and apparel, used focus groups to gain insight into older persons' perceptions of problems and apparel preferences. Participants were asked to examine drawings, pictures and samples of different styles and rank them according to the likelihood of being purchased. The more popular styles were then adapted to the known preferences of the fashion-conscious older adult.

Distribution is of particular importance in selling to seniors; most older shoppers rank store reputation above brand or label in their apparel purchase decisions. Thus, manufacturers are eager to place merchandise in well-known stores that cater to older clientele. Sears Roebuck and the May Company, for example, have established clubs and fashion shows to appeal to older shoppers. Bloomingdales, Marshall Field's and Bonwit Teller are major department stores which carry Janet Sartin and other cosmetic lines and apparel aimed at the older woman. Allied Stores Corporation and The Limited are two of the many stores featuring larger-sized fashionable clothing for older shoppers.

Since many fashion-conscious older adults are likely to attend social events and community activities, fashion shows are a popular form of promotion for retailers that cater to older consumers. Many large department stores have special in-store fashion shows that feature apparel for mature men and women. Some stores hold their fashion shows at Senior Centers and other locations with a large number of elderly.

Blue Jeans

Heavy blue denim started out as workclothes fabric of farmers and construction crews. After World War II, fashion designers started working the material into pants for the younger set and the rest is history. Jeans have become the uniform and the symbol of young America.

But in an aging America, where blue jeans sales have dropped from over 500 million pairs of jeans in 1980 to 400 million in 1988, manufacturers are seeking ways to continue to sell jeans to their now older customers. But how do you appeal to the senior set with their preference for softer material and looser fit without turning off the younger generation?

Advertising Age asked three ad agencies experienced in advertising to the mature market to tackle the problem and create an ad campaign for a fictional brand of blue jeans targeted to adults over 50. The results were reported in a special "Maturity Marketing" supplement of the trade journal.

Cadwell Davis Partners named their brand "First Jeaneration" and advertised the product with a photo of an older female model in a rural setting wearing jeans and a cowboy hat. The company's president Frankie Cadwell describes the image created in the ad as "a statement of character. She's someone people of all ages can respect and gravitate to."

In creating an ad for their Surefits jeans (". . . Jeans for grownups"), Primelife, a California agency that specializes in marketing to older adults, reasoned that most mature consumers perceive themselves as 10 to 15 years younger than their chronological age and chose to show models of various ages wearing their jeans. The copy reads, "Who says jeans have to be a fading memory? 'Surefits' for the way you play today." A simple design, larger typeface and plenty of space between lines makes the ad easy to read.

Jordan, McGrath, Case & Taylor created an ad that featured Wilford Brimley, known for his oatmeal commercials and fast becoming the unoffical spokesman for the senior generation. The ad for the fictional "Ranch Hand Jeans" features a close-in shot of Wilford on horseback. The headline, "Real men don't wear tight jeans." The agency's vice-chairman Mal MacDougall says that the ad celebrates comfortable jeans. He believes that "somebody ought to come out with this product."

Designing and selling clothes to the most elderly of the older generation is a specialty within the apparel industry. A company called "Silver Threads," that caters to elderly men and women who live in nursing homes, is celebrating its eleventh year in business. It works this way: Traveling vans set up a one-day shopping center within the facility and residents, families and staff are able to browse and shop for clothing, undergarments and accessories.

Martin Misiaszek, the founder and head of "Silver Threads," says that "Even in a nursing home environment, we try to bring in a contemporary look. When 'Urban Cowboy' was a hit movie we sold a lot of snapfront cowboy shirts. Now we're selling more jogging outfits than any other item in the clothing line." He says that jogging outfits are comfortable and contemporary, and the staff enjoys seeing residents in up-beat apparel. "Silver Threads" won't sell black or very dark colored item because they're considered depressing. The challenge to manufacturers, he says, "is to make adaptive clothing attractive and, at the same time, keep costs down."

Other examples of manufacturers accommodating the needs of seniors: Levi Strausss manufactures a special line of fuller cut clothing and jeans more suited to the figures of older people. "Sophisticated Seniors," manufactures a line of lively apparel for older women and uses nursing home residents to model their clothes.

Older Women—"The New Gold Market"

The stereotyped image of the female apparel customer over

50 persists as that of a conservative, traditional, price-concerned shopper primarily seeking intimate apparel, dusters and pants suits. This image is breaking down, however, as marketers begin to understand that women aged 50 and over are a dynamic, vibrant group who have different lifestyles and diverging apparel wants and needs. To bring this market into focus, Celanese Fibers commissioned, "The New Gold Market," a comprehensive study of women 50 to 65 based on a national consumer survey and Gallup Poll interviews.

The demographic outlook for the "Gold Market" female segment of the population, between 1985 and the year 2000, is as follows:

	1985	*2000*	*Difference*
Total Women 50–65 (millions)	18.3	23.0	+ 25.6 percent
Women 50–55	6.0	9.7	+ 61.6
Women 55–60	6.3	7.5	+ 19.6
Women 60–65	6.0	5.8	- 3.4

Among the most interesting of "The New Gold Market" findings are the data on working women:

	Share of Working Women
Total U.S.	68 percent
Women 50–55	59 percent
Women 55–60	50 percent
Women 60–65	34 percent

Almost half of the women 50 to 65 surveyed are working, and among the youngest sub-segment (50 to 55) almost 60 percent are working. The company estimates that by 1995 about two-thirds of the 50 to 55 year olds will be working full or part-time and that, "our marketing programs have to be strongly geared to the needs of the working woman."

Specifically, these needs were broken down by the three age groups studied:

The 50-55 sub-segment: "They are most likely to be working, are better educated and have above average disposable incomes . . . more style conscious and want well known brand names or designer labels . . . above average buyers of skirts, slacks, dresses, skirt suits, blouses."

The 55-60 sub-segment: "Women in this age sector are in transition from a working environment to a more leisured environment . . . styling tends to be conservative for sportswear/working clothes but more experimental and fashion forward for leisurewear . . . above average customers for skirts, slacks, pant suits, warm-up suits, skirt suits, dresses."

The 60-65 sub-segment: "Still a very affluent market with per capita income 22 percent above national average. This is an affluent travel and leisure group preparing for full retirement. Primarily interested in leisurewear—stylish for socializing and simpler for home . . . prime customers for moderately priced leisurewear, particularly, pant suits, slacks, intimate apparel, sleepwear."

"The Gold Market Report" offers the following suggestions for attracting the older woman customer:

- Store catalogs should use models and apparel appropriate for this market.
- Showcasing of merchandise with special fit and color coordination could stimulate in-store sales.
- "Customer traffic could be improved by developing in-store promotions that are sensitive to their needs, but are not offensive to their sensibilities. Such as exercise programs, beauty care programs, diet programs, travel and financial services and gardening and flower arrangement lectures."

While the study finds that speciality stores, more than department stores, are perceived to be doing a better job of catering to the needs of the upscale older customer, some department stores, J.C. Penney, for example, has tried to relate to older customers. The company created a special lifestyle classification linked to "dressing attitude, not age." Barbara Bierman, merchandise publicity manager for Penney, says that "As this Baby Boom moves along and accounts for such a large portion of the market, we can chart their preferences and act to fill their needs."

Marketing Communications magazine quoted apparel industry leaders on the subject of older customers. Ray Sessler, president of Leslie Fay II, a company division created to satisfy the new fashion needs of older women: "She may be larger, but she doesn't want to wear something that's old-looking. Stores are spending more money in this market, and they understand, as we do, that this woman is more fashion-conscious than ever." Bernard Blue, manufacturer of moderately priced clothing for older women: "Number one, I think this woman is looking for fashion; number two, price. The older woman is looking for something that can worn for a longer period of time, something that is not going to make her look like she's trying to chop off 30 years."

Seniors and Big Ticket Purchases

With their greater discretionary income, seniors are in a position to afford many of the big ticket products that make life easier and more fun. Whether they be such practical items as microwave ovens, sewing machines and vacuum cleaners, or leisure items such as pianos, boats and movie cameras, seniors make up an important part of the market for major purchases.

A study of big ticket purchasing patterns, conducted by Yankelovich Skelly and White for Ziff-Davis, publisher of such up-scale special magazines as *Popular Photography*, *Yachting* and *Psychology Today*, points out some interesting differences between the purchasing behavior and attitudes of seniors versus younger age segments:

• Big ticket purchases that 50+ adults believe to be necessary are considered a luxury by younger adults.

• While none of the age groups studied could be classified as brand loyal in the big ticket area, more repeat purchases by younger buyers involved a brand change than the "repeats" bought by older buyers.

• In measuring the recall ability of consumers exposed to brand advertising, there was no discernible difference between age groups.

• Older consumers place more emphasis on the fact that the brand be one which they have heard of or is nationally advertised.

• Older consumers spend less time shopping and deliberating about big ticket purchases (four weeks or more for 42 percent of buyers under 35, while only 31 percent of older buyers spent that much time considering their purchase).

Much of this data reflects the fact that the older consumer is more likely to be buying the big ticket item as a replacement, or as a gift while the younger adult buyer "just needed or wanted one." It also shows the older person as an experienced and brand-conscious consumer.

When it comes to big ticket items, sometimes the older generation will surprise you. One doesn't think of the mature individual as a prime prospect for electronic items but the Electronics Industries Association tells us that 45 percent of people aged 50 to 59 own Video Cassette Recorders, a percentage equal to that of all households nationwide. Approximately 19 percent of adults over 60 own VCRs. In the 1990s, when the first of the baby boomers enter their fifties, they bring with them their interest in high-tech electronic equipment and other types of products not tradionally associated with the mature market. Marketers need to be aware of this to adjust their strategies accordingly.

The Automobile Buyer

If it's true that Americans have a love affair with their automobiles, it is a love affair that extends far into the later years. Mature customers are far and away the best prospects for the luxury cars and the extra options that are so profitable to manufacturers and auto dealers. Approximately 56 percent of all new car purchases are made by heads of household who are 50 and over, and the cars they buy are more expensive than those purchased by younger groups.

As the data on page 169 indicates, 76 percent of older car buyers prefer automobiles "Made in America," versus 54 percent of the youngest adult group. In addition to favoring American automobiles, seniors want and can afford larger cars and they have traditionally been the major market for them. In 1988, two-thirds of domestic luxury-models such as the Cadillac Coupe de Ville and Lincoln Town Car were sold to buyers over age 55. Among the other brands favored by seniors are Buick, Oldsmobile, Ford and Chevrolet, particularly the roomier, larger models with reputations for dependability and safety.

Studies by Detroit-based Maritz Marketing Research indicate that the average large-car buyer is age 60, with an annual income of $42,000. Seven out of every 10 of the car buyers are married and only one in 10 has children living at home.

More than most other products, automobiles reflect the personality, status and consumer behavior of its owner and are strongly associated with particular lifestyles and age groups. For many years, Oldsmobile has been perceived as an older person's car, and even though today's Olds is a very different car than it used to be and has the style and performance that appeals to younger buyers, the perception of Oldsmobile as an older person's automobile is difficult to shake. Even the older adult car buyer doesn't want to be seen driving "an old man's car."

In 1988, General Motor's Oldsmobile division launched the biggest ad effort in its history to establish a new image. The campaign, created by the Leo Burnett advertising agency, proclaims "This is not your father's Oldsmobile. This is a new generation of Olds." To ensure that its appeal bridges the generation gap, the company uses two or three generations of famous families, each chosen to fit the image and selling position of the car. TV and film stars and other famous families appear in its print and television commercials— Star Trek's William Shatner, astronaut Scott Carpenter and the granddaughter of Norman Rockwell are among the personalities used to promote a "new generation of Olds."

Besides attracting younger car buyers, this campaign is designed to change the image of the car for the mature adult who doesn't want to be stigmatized by driving an old man's car. There's a lesson here for marketers wooing the mature market. When you identify your product too closely with age, you run the risk of turning off the very people for whom the product was designed. Instead, sell the features that older persons are interested in (roomy, comfortable, reliable) without being age specific.

As the automobile industry plans for the future, it looks to the marketplace for trends. The data on the opposite page is based on studies of the number and types of autos purchased by various age groups and the factors involved in the purchase decision. They provide useful guidelines for auto manufacturers and dealers interested in pursuing the mature market.

New Car Purchases by Age Category, Domestic vs. Foreign and Factors Considered Extremely/Very Important in Purchase Decision

Price of auto	AGE:	*18-24*	*25-34*	*35-54*	*55+*
Under $10,000		45 %	34%	24%	17%
$10,000 to $14,990		45	50	51	53
$15,000 and over		10	16	25	30
American cars		54%	54%	64%	76%
European		4	6	7	3
Japanese		41	38	29	20

Factors important to decision	*18-24*	*25-34*	*35-54*	*55+*
Prestige/image	42%	28%	25%	23%
Made by an American Company	30	32	43	63
Previous experience with dealer	24	22	29	42
Dealer reputation	55	52	63	77
Convenient dealer location	35	39	46	62
Interest rate offer	49	44	40	27
Safety features	58	62	68	82
Previous experience with make	32	36	41	56

Source: Newsweek 1986 Report of New Car Buyers.

CHAPTER EIGHT

FINANCIAL SERVICES

So many changes have occurred in the financial services industry that many consider it nothing less than a financial services revolution. Advances in technology, deregulation, diversification of product lines and the merging of many financial services giants have changed forever who sells what to whom. As a result of these changes, stockbrokers are allowing customers to write checks against their accounts and banks are managing investment accounts and selling mutual funds. This is just one of the many examples in which it is difficult to distinguish between the financial services offered to the consumer by banks, savings and loan associations, credit unions, securities brokerage houses, mutual funds and insurance companies.

Add to that the mind-boggling proliferation of services and products (IRAs and Keoghs, money market funds and commodity funds, zero coupon bonds and single-payment annuities, to name just a few) combined with increased competition, merger and acquisition activity, "one-stop shopping" financial services and the opportunity it offers for cross-selling by such financial conglomerates as American Express, Merrill Lynch, Prudential and Sears, and you can see how different things are today from when today's senior first started using financial services.

Considering the ease with which financial institutions

change flags, it is no wonder that there is less customer loyalty today. Customers will walk away from a bank or an insurance agent where they have done business for many years if they can find a better deal elsewhere. Even those older persons who would remain loyal are forced to look elsewhere when their financial situation changes radically or when they relocate to another state. Today's older, more sophisticated financial services customer is aware of the alternatives (even though he or she, like people of all ages, may not necessarily understand them) and tends to shop around.

Consequently, financial institutions have to find more effective ways to woo the senior market. Banks can no longer count on an individual's business just because they are close to the individual's home. Investors are buying CDs from thrifts far from home in order to get better yields. Insurance companies can't depend on the glib pitch of their salesman to sell their policies; millions of dollars in insurance premiums are generated each year by direct mail advertising. Stock brokers can't rely on old telephone techniques pushing today's hot stock; they need to start relating to the changing needs of their aging customers.

The competition for business between banks, insurance companies and stockbrokers is being waged in several areas. Price of services, the choice of product and service offered, quality of service and convenience are some of the factors that are most important to older adults.

The larger that financial institutions grow, with several divisions and many branches, the more difficult it is to offer the kind of personal, individual service that attracts older persons. And yet, considering the range of choices one has to make in handling financial matters and the amount of explaining those choices require, that difficulty will have to be overcome and innovative solutions to the product-service gap will be required in order to stay abreast of the competition.

The Mature Investor

Financially secure seniors control an enormous amount of the accumulated wealth. Census Bureau statistics indicate that the median net worth of persons over 65 is almost double that of the general population, a fact of galvanizing interest to purveyors of financial services. Chicago-based Kemper Financial Services ran a demographic analysis of its mutual fund shareholders and was "startled at what a terrific group the elderly are," says Stephen Gibson, the company's first vice-president for marketing. The research showed that the company's older mutual-funds investors invested more and stayed in the fund longer than their younger shareholders. Subsequently, Kemper stepped up its sales efforts to seniors, as have many other financial services.

For a profile of today's financially secure mature investor, marketers can look to places like Leisure World, a retirement community in Laguna Hills, California. While the 21,000 people who live in Leisure World (average age, 76) don't think of themselves as rich, it would be fair to assume a certain level of financial comfort. How else would you explain a community of this size with 26 savings and loan associations, 15 banks, over a dozen stock brokerage firms and untold numbers of investment advisers?

Writing in Barron's, a Dow-Jones financial publication, Sanford L. Jacobs found three main streams to the current of life in Leisure World—recreation, self-improvement and investment. He reported that most seniors living there "are keenly interested in investing, eager to learn how their assets could be most effectively placed. But actually getting those assets into a particular investment depends on how successful the seller is in tailoring his marketing to the particular needs, likes and dislikes of seniors."

Like most communities of this kind, Leisure World residents are flooded with appeals from financial services through advertisements, seminars and telephone solicitations. Investment marketers favor the educational approach for this market and seminars are a proven method of reaching seniors, particularly if refreshments are served. Every week residents are invited to lunch and dinner presentations by the local Prudential-Bache Securities. In his Barron's article, Jacobs explained why the firm's branch manager believes that seniors are different from younger investors: "They like to take delivery of their stock certificates, prefer doing business face to face rather than over the phone and relentlessly look for income, preferably tax sheltered income."

According to Mr. Jacobs, "Anyone who hopes to do business with senior investors has to remember that they are the survivors of the worst economic cataclysm ever to strike the nation . . . Brokers here do little business in hot, sexy little over-the-counter stocks or the wilder limited partnerships. They make most of their living on municipal bonds, mutual funds, CDs, money-management and financial planning services, and the bluest of the blue chips. Caution is the watchword in Leisure World, where memories are long."

What Senior Investors Own

Average amount owned, (percent of age group who own this asset), by age of head of household.

Asset Age:	45–64	65–74	75 +
Stocks/Mutual Funds	$ 69,392 (22%)	$226,160 (23%)	$324,914 (11%)
Money Market/CDs	29,341 (31%)	57,814 (43%)	43,935 (39%)
Bonds	26,214 (23%)	101,684 (21%)	70,846 (10%)
Checking/ Savings Accounts	7,816 (87%)	12,281 (90%)	16,875 (87%)
IRAs/Keoghs	20,302 (41%)	57,675 (18%)	62,353 (5%)
Profit Sharing/Thrifts	43,704 (18%)	149,147 (2%)	34,430 (1%)
Life Ins. cash value	8,955 (47%)	13,380 (40%)	3,611 (32%)
Other financial assets	144,712 (6%)	170,333 (8%)	191,168 (4%)
Principal residence	88,332 (77%)	79,806 (82%)	53,956 (76%)
Other properties	119,802 (26%)	119,802 (27%)	117,867 (18%)
Business assets	261,325 (15%)	540,983 (8%)	283,178 (4%)
Net Worth	$ 152,391	$ 249,844	$ 135,516

Source: Survey of Consumer Finances, 1986, Federal Reserve Board.

Investments

One week after the stock market crash on Black Monday, October 19, 1987, *The Wall Street Journal* carried an article with the headline: "For Many Retirees, Crash Isn't a Disaster." The article offered insight to the investment behavior of seniors:

> "Retirees living on fixed incomes generally take pains to insure that those incomes don't become unfixed. Because they tend to avoid speculative investments, financial specialists say many retirees didn't benefit extensively from the stock market's huge advance of recent years. But they also haven't been clobbered by the past week's huge retreats."

The huge losses avoided by many older investors during the crash of '87 confirmed the protective wisdom that comes with age. Despite the temptation to make a killing in a raging bull market, most mature investors continued to put their money into such safe, low risk investments as CDs, high-quality bonds and government securities. Almost everyone past the age of 60 has to come to grips with the fact that their future financial security depends in large measure on their skill in managing what they already have.

Older investors who are willing and able to accept the risks of stock ownership in pursuit of greater rewards are nevertheless influenced by their strong memories of the Depression. The Journal quotes a Sunrise, Florida retiree: "In 1929, we didn't have any money, period. Going through the Depression gave us a better sense of value. You don't invest everything you possess. And you don't spend everything you possess."

While older adults are careful, conservative investors, they are receptive to investment ideas that are appropriate to their stage of life. That means less interest in high-risk stocks, futures and options, tax shelters and limited partnerships and a greater interest in conservative, blue-chip stock, high grade bonds and CDs. Nevertheless, seniors remain

good customers for stockbrokers and other financial services. Over 25 percent of the respondents to a *Modern
Maturity* survey of their readers have an account with a
stock brokerage firm; approximately 16 percent had security
portfolios worth $100,000 or more, with the average valued
at $97,300.

Three out of every four respondents to the reader survey own one or more of the following types of securities:

	Owned by
Money market funds	49.9 percent
Stocks (common and preferred)	36.5
U.S. Savings Bonds	23.8
Mutual funds (stocks or bonds)	18.6
Municipal bonds	9.5
U.S. Treasury Notes	6.7
Corporate bonds	5.1
Other U.S. government bonds	4.4

Collections

Silver and silver coins	20.9 percent
Art and antiques	16.1
Collectibles	15.4
Gold and gold coins	7.8

Banking

A story going around bank circles: It seems that this elderly
gentleman would show up at the bank every day precisely
at half past noon and again at 2:30 in the afternoon to get
into his Safe Deposit Box. After many months of this
routine, the bank manager, overcome with curiosity, asked
the gentleman why he visited his Safe Deposit Box every
day at half-past noon. "Why, it's to get money for lunch,"
he explained. "Ah," said the bank manager, "now I understand. But tell me, why do you come back again at 2:30?"

"Oh, that," the man replied, "It's to put back the change."

Even though bankers recognize the humorous exaggeration, many see it as a fairly accurate description of their elderly clientele—eccentric, parsimonious, and with plenty of time to spend handling their finances. A banker friend of mine, however, reacted to the story this way: "That story describes a kind of person and not an age group. Most of the older customers at my bank are pretty busy people and don't have the time to visit the bank often. Some even bank exclusively by mail. Still, seniors are our most valued customers and if they want to visit the bank ten times a day, I'm happy to see them. Every visit is another opportunity to sell one of the bank's services."

Bank customers over 55 control 80 percent of the dollars in savings institutions and most of the dollars in key account or private banking portfolios; they maintain checking-account balances that average 25 percent to 50 percent higher than the norm. Seniors are a bank's most reliable, loyal and stable customers and the bank that builds a large customer list of older adults enjoys a strong base for current business and future growth. Banks enjoy a competitive advantage over other financial services seeking this business by providing those services that seniors care about most—guaranteed safe investments, high rates of return, trouble-free checking accounts and personal attention. The large and growing number of affluent seniors and the increased competition from other types of financial services for their business make it more important than ever that banks reexamine their marketing efforts to older customers.

Jim Schneider, an Oak Brook, Illinois consultant, and previously in sales and marketing at First National Bank of Chicago and Security Savings of Milwaukee, believes that the senior market offers banks huge profit potential, but few bankers are using what they know about seniors to sell them more of the bank's services. His position is strengthened by a recent American Banker magazine report in which one-third of the adults surveyed said that they prefer to do all their financial business—checking, savings, investment, etc.—with one financial company. Of those surveyed, 59 percent gave convenience as the reason, 30 percent said it was "more efficient, less risky, and 13 percent cited more personal and better service as the reason.

Bank personnel dealing with seniors need to be sensitive to seniors' needs and not to put off by their occasional slowness and talkativeness. Because banking requires "relationship," the key is in getting information, not giving it. Customers need plenty of time to talk, then recommendations can be made based on a solid understanding of their needs.

Trust, personal relationships and performance are important factors to older bank customers. The older and more cautious the buyer, the more important trust becomes. The privacy and caring relationship implied by private banking are strong incentives in winning and keeping their business.

Mr. Schneider counsels that retail banking personnel, particularly young tellers and personal bankers, need special training to understand the importance of senior customers and "they need assertiveness training because they are sometimes intimidated by the directness, experience and shopping knowledge of older customers."

Seniors want more assurances than do other customers. Older adults are more likely to be concerned about the financial integrity of savings institutions because they remember firsthand the "bank holidays" and the bank closings during the depression of the thirties. They want to know about the people and the organization that will stand behind the products and services they purchase.

Seniors also rely heavily on the opinion of peers. They want to share their buying experience with others. Word of mouth, and selling through a senior network, is like adding a free sales force. In a Bank Marketing article, Jim Schneider says, "You'll get their networks buzzing if you involve seniors in helping other seniors. When I was marketing director for Security Savings in Milwaukee, we were the first financial institution in America to use a steering committee of seniors to make decisions for our senior program. Its outreach was a phenomenal success."

He believes that it is important that bankers recognize the diverse interests and needs of the different segments of the mature market and that they recognize that people differ more in personality as they age, "with some becoming more passive and dependent and others reorganizing their lives and increasing their activities."

In any case, seniors offer infinite possibilities for cross merchandising and are potential customers for many of the banks growing menu of services—checking and savings accounts, trust department services, personal loans, home and condominium mortgages, reverse mortgages, investment services, CDs and money market funds, NOW accounts (interest paying checking accounts), estate planning and management, IRA and Keogh accounts, automatic deposit of Social-Security checks and automatic bill payment.

Bankers who take their time to develop a rapport with seniors and to understand their needs and earn their trust and respect, will be more likely to win their considerable investment business.

A recent article in the *Journal of Retail Banking*, by John J. Burnett and Robert Wilkes reported the findings of a study sponsored by the University of South Carolina. The findings provide insight to the banking patterns of older bank customers at different stages of their maturity. The numbers represent the percent of those in that age category who responded or behaved in the manner suggested.

Banking Behavior	% 45–54	% 55–64	% 65+
Have checking account	71.8	62.1	46.8
Have NOW account	17.7	23.2	52.1
Have personal loan	24.6	16.3	11.7
Rent safe deposit box	38.3	43.1	58.5
Have savings account	91.5	90.5	90.4
Have insurance	89.4	86.4	81.9
Own stocks	43.6	44.8	58.5
Own bonds	11.9	17.2	26.6
Most checks written	11.9	10.3	5.3
Highest daily balances in checking	7.7	6.9	8.5
Have bank money market account	19.7	19.8	41.5
Have bank charge card	70.4	56.9	59.7
Use bank direct deposit	22.5	20.6	27.6
Have bank mortgage loan	21.3	6.9	3.2

Bank-Sponsored Senior Clubs

Some of the most successful market strategies for banks are built around innovative "senior club" concepts. One such program, the American Patriots Club, sponsored by the The American Savings & Loan Association of California, boasts a membership of over 120,000 members throughout 187 branches. The club was one of the sponsors of a recent Los Angeles Senior Expo attended by over 50,000 older adults. A single, 30-second television spot, showing seniors tap dancing and singing the praises of the S&L, was credited with bringing in $30 million in new accounts in one day. American Savings & Loan also promotes its American Patriots Club through direct mail and print advertising.

In the midwest, Talman Home Federal Savings and Loan Association offers Club Discovery membership to customers 55 and older who maintain $1,000 in a passbook account and $5,000 in CDs. The club has about 60,000 members from the Chicago area. Members are encouraged to use community rooms at two main branches. They're invited to participate in nearly 100 trips and special events scheduled throughout the year, and they receive a quarterly newsletter listing the club's activities. Scheduled tours include Munich, West Germany, an autumn tour of New England, the Florida Keys and Mackinac Island in Michigan. Events sponsored by Talman for Club Discovery include seminars and lectures on consumer affairs and medical topics, as well as dinner-theatre evenings.

One of the oldest senior clubs is sponsored by Central Fidelity in Virginia. The bank's ten-year-old senior club, Focus 60, has 40,000 members and is free to persons 60 and over who maintain a balance of $2,500 in any one of the bank's savings, checking or IRA accounts. Benefits include free checking services, travelers checks, estate planning counseling, free storage of wills and free notary service. There is a Focus 60 specialist in every one of the bank's 167 branches to assist members and coordinate the numerous social events and travel tours sponsored by the club.

In 1987, Central Fidelity conducted 52 trips with 1,419 participants, sponsored 44 seminars, held 54 social events with 4,000 participants, and conducted over fifty internal "sensitivity training" sessions for bank employees. In the same year, the program brought in 1,755 new accounts and ended the year with 35,000 seniors as customers, representing 32 percent of the banks total retail deposits. Assistant Vice-President, Janice Quinn characterizes Focus 60 members as "big deposit, low loan" customers, an observation echoed by many bankers with a senior clientele. Central Fidelity's 13 consecutive years of increased earnings is unmatched by any other Virginia bank-holding company, a record that is largely attributable to successful programs such as Focus 60.

Programs of this kind have proved so successful at bringing in profitable business, and in creating good will among older adults, that the idea has spread from coast to coast. Banks and thrifts contemplating such clubs are advised to employ a mature individual to help develop the program and commit adequate resources to advertise it effectively. At some point, word of mouth will take over and put the program over the top.

While senior clubs have proved to be an effective marketing tool and enable banks to make a genuine contribution to the community, the club format may not be practical for many banks and thrifts. Those institutions may, however, benefit by employing some of the ideas generated by these clubs:

- No-postage-required envelopes for mailing in deposits.
- Special 800 lines to answer inquiries.
- Automatic deposit of Social Security checks.
- Automatic bill-paying services.
- Free will storage.
- Telephone transfer from one account to another.
- Free or special discounts for Safe Deposit Boxes.
- Discount coupons for movies, restaurants or local merchants.

- Free notary service.
- Interest rate bonus on CD purchases.

Insurance

In recent years, the emphasis in life insurance purchases by adults 50 and over has shifted from whole life and endowment policies, which combine insurance and investment, to term and group insurance. They have followed the advice of the stock, bond and mutual fund salesmen to "buy term and invest the difference." There has also been a conceptual shift in the purpose of life insurance and people have favored the kind of insurance that they don't have to die to enjoy.

Thus we see increased interest in annuities and guaranteed return insurance policies. As more and more of these products become available, the insurance industry faces greater competition from investment vehicles that meet the needs of an older, more financially savvy customer. Today's seniors, with their higher level of education and many years of experience in managing their financial affairs, tend to pay closer attention to the complex array of insurance and financial planning products available.

Ocassional setbacks in the stock market have taken some of the steam out of the "buy term and invest the difference" approach and conservative savings plans are once again in vogue. Insurance marketing should now be stressing personal savings, guaranteed returns and safety. As life expectancy lengthens, a larger and more secure financial cushion will be required to maintain a comfortable standard of living in retirement. This provides the insurance business with an opportunity to develop products and services that will meet the demand for conservative employment of accumulated assets.

Health Insurance

Modern health insurance started in the 1930s with Blue Cross, and similar associations, providing private group and individual health insurance. In reality, such insurance was a form of prepayment for, and protection against, hospital and medical costs. In recent years, new forms of protection, particularly major medical expense plans, long-term disability coverage and dental insurance, have grown rapidly and health insurance has emerged as a formidable growth industry.

Many men and women in their fifties are covered for health insurance by group or employer-sponsored policies or by individually purchased health insurance. In their mid-60s, when retired men and women become eligible for Social Security, they are entitled to government Medicare benefits. Since Medicare covers only part of the medical expenses involved in an illness, the private sector stepped in to provide a special kind of supplementary policy, frequently referred to as "Medigap" insurance, to protect against unusually high medical expenses. The market for health services insurance to supplement Medicare is booming and the competition among insurers to provide seniors with such protection has grown quite lively.

In addition to "Medigap" insurance, the market for private long term care insurance is growing at a remarkable rate. A survey, by the Health Insurance Association of America (HIAA), finds that the number of companies selling long-term care insurance has increased more than 6 times over the number in 1984 to more than 105 companies in 1988. In a 21-month period ending in December of 1988, the number of individuals, who purchased private long-term care insurance, increased almost three times to more than 1.1 million persons.

With one out of every four adults over 50 considering themselves as "more at risk than the average person" in the possibility of needing long term care at some time in the future, it is logical that seniors are the major purchasers of such insurance. How are these policies marketed? Twenty two policies were sold on an individual basis, seven were sold to individuals who were members of various organizations. Nineteen of the companies sold their long term care insurance policies using their own agents or independent brokers, while six used agents and mail solicitations. Four companies sold their products only through the mail.

The present 1.1 million policyholders represents a very small portion of the potential market for such policies. Susan van Gelder, associate director of policy and research for the HIAA, estimates that 40 percent, of the nation's 29 million seniors 65 and over, could afford private long term care insurance and could meet the underwriting requirements.

CHAPTER NINE
SENIOR HOUSING

Most Americans start out in life living at home with parents and then follow a typical housing cycle: Between their early 20s to mid-30s they move into their own place. If and when they marry, they may move to a rental apartment or a small house, and when the children come along the route usually leads to home ownership, sometimes in the city but often in the suburbs. When our typical couple reaches their 50s, the children move out to start a housing cycle of their own, leaving their parents—now seniors—as empty nesters.

This broad generalization has become less valid in this age of changing lifestyles and cultural diversity, but it does describe the typical housing "passages" of today's seniors when they were younger. After age 50, there is little in the way of a discernible pattern. Some older men and women choose to stay where they are, while others decide to move elsewhere, perhaps to a smaller place. When they become empty nesters, many older couples sell their house and move to an apartment.

After the retirement lunch and the gold watch, many older men and women move into mature adult communities (also called retirement communities) in their general area. Others, lured by a friendlier climate and leisure lifestyle, pick up stakes and relocate in another part of the country, usually the Sun Belt. Those who move are the major targets of the purveyors of senior housing, they are the preference driven prospects for housing. In their later years, many of these seniors may have to make housing decisions based on need rather than preference, but while they are healthy and active their behavior as housing consumers is determined by their choice of lifestyle.

Significant life changes create a shift from preferred-housing to need-housing which combines shelter with medical services and assistance. Such change can be caused by any one or a combination of problems—impaired mobility, poor health, loss of a spouse, change in economic status, or any number of conditions "that flesh is heir to." For those unable to live independently and without some form of medical care, a new set of options present themselves and, once again, the choice is influenced by the individual's physical and financial status. Among the options are the various types of facilities which provide housing plus assistance, supervision, nursing and medical care in many different combinations and for different size pocketbooks.

Even though men and women in their 50s and 60s are more likely to be part of the market for traditional shelter, many individuals in this younger-old group opt for congregate or retirement-type housing near their current home or in the Sun Belt. For the most part, however, it is only when they reach their late 60s and after that they become prime prospects for the features offered by senior housing developers.

The main reasons people over 55 give for moving include such practical matters as reducing expenses, preference for a smaller home and eliminating the need to make repairs. Primary motivations for moving are followed closely by the wish not to be a burden on the family, moving closer to relatives and moving to improve the climate they live in.

These findings are from a research study sponsored by The National Association for Senior Living Industries, a not-for-profit network of businesses and professionals involved in meeting the shelter, health, services and consumer product needs of the older population. The study, entitled

SENIOR HOUSING CYCLE

Choices for Senior Couple,
Empty Nest, Living in Detached Single Family House.

Option I — Stay where they are (age in place).

Option II — Relocate within same general area.

a) Buy or rent smaller house.

b) Buy a condominium.

c) Rent an apartment.

d) Move to a senior community within general area.

Option III — migrate to Sun Belt after retirement.

a) Live independently in house or apartment.

b) Move to a retirement community.

Options after Crisis (physical limitations become acute, loss of spouse, change in finances, caretaker no longer available, etc.).

a) Continue to live at home with visiting health care.

b) Move in with children or other relatives.

c) Move to a senior center with health care facilities.

d) Move to a long term health care facility.

e) Enter a nursing home.

LAVOA (Lifestyles and Values of Older Adults), was conducted to give "designers, producers, marketers, and deliverers of products and services greater insight into older adults' attitudes, needs, and consumer decision-making behavior." Among the reasons for moving less mentioned in the study, but relevant to marketers of senior housing, are—to get help taking care of themselves, to live closer to shops and to achieve a new lifestyle. It is worth noting that the 55 and over group were more likely to include "reduce living expenses," "have a smaller house" and "live in a better climate," while the 65 to 74 respondents are most likely to move in order to eliminate home maintenance and repairs. Renters, as opposed to homeowners, are more likely to move in order to be in a safer neighborhood.

Among other significant findings of the LAVOA study . . .

- Senior homeowners are willing to become future apartment dwellers or owners of smaller, easier-to-maintain single-family units. About one-half of the seniors who expressed an interest in moving said that they would prefer to move to a single-family house, but more than one-third are interested in apartments and condominiums.

- Housing decisions by mature adults are influenced by whether an individual is autonomous or independent. Independent and active seniors are likely to pass up supportive housing arrangements like group housing senior complexes or living with relatives. Dependent seniors, however, look forward to living with family members or in an environment that includes services.

- By using psychological analysis, LAVOA tried to pinpoint diverging preferences in the senior housing market. It finds, for example, that extroverts are likely to prefer congregate housing, which includes social activities, while introverts are more likely to choose group housing and retirement communities.

- Self-indulgent individuals will avoid low-status surroundings, while self-denying personalities will actively seek out such housing. These attitudes also determine moves to better climates and more expensive mature housing. "Self-indulgents" are more likely to be married, and to have higher incomes. Withdrawn, or rigid individuals are likely to be anxious, depressed and avoid social contact. Outgoing "explorer" types, seniors likely to be highly educated and financially secure, tend to seek out housing that matches their personalities.

For seniors contemplating a change—whether driven by desire or need—the options are many, and the competition among the various kinds of housing developers is keen. Among the choices open to the mature adult are . . .

Adult Communities or Retirement Communities. These are complexes of permanent dwelling communities for older adults, ranging in size from as few as 100 units to as many as 45,000—the average is in the 4,000 to 5,000 range. Communities of this type are concentrated in the Sun Belt states, Arizona, California, Florida and Texas. They are usually located some distance from the center of town on a tract of undeveloped land originally bought at a highly favorable price. Some of the larger adult communities and retirement centers, Sun City in Arizona and Leisure World in California, for example, become virtually self-contained towns, with their own community centers, clubhouses, and the latest in sports and recreational facilities. Some have health care facilities and the larger developments have their own shopping centers. Communities of this type are designed for seniors who have the funds to afford the purchase of a condominium unit and a comfortable retirement income to pay the monthly fees for recreation and maintenance. Bus or van transportation may be provided, but the automobile is still the way that most of the residents of adult communities get around. Marketers responsible for condominium sales in these communities can offer a carefree, secure, clean and well-ordered environment. Their best prospects are friendly, outgoing, and physically active seniors in relatively good health who are financially well-to-do.

Congregate housing (CH) or Life-care community (LCC). T h i s type of senior housing differs from retirement communities in size, location, average age of residents, and services offered. Unlike the large retirement communities, congregate residences and life-care communities average 150 units, with a maximum of about 350. Many congregate housing and life-care communities are located in or near a town. Facilities of this kind are located throughout the country, as opposed to retirement communities which are concentrated in the Sunbelt states. Congregate housing and life-care communities provide recreational facilities but they also provide life-support services such as meals, housekeeping and emergency medical care. Life-care communities provide complete health care, including long-term custodial nursing care if needed.

Mobile Homes. Sometimes referred to as "manufactured housing," most mobile home parks can be found in the Western and Southern states While most mobile home parks are not age specific, some have a preponderance of older persons and house large numbers of residence who are 60 and older. Mobile home parks are chosen by older people, usually couples, of moderate means who like a community environment; they are more age-integrated and less expensive than a retirement community, but include amenities like clubhouses.

Housing for Independent, Active Seniors

The statistics tells us that most seniors prefer not to move. Consequently, the proportion of the senior population that constitute "good prospects" for housing developers is not large, but the number of seniors is so great that even a small percent of the total represents a vast housing market. The emergence of senior communities and retirement developments and the large number of people moving into them, provide ample evidence of a substantial and lucrative market. So much so, that companies from different types of businesses—many like Chubb Insurance Company and Avon Products, companies far removed from the traditional housing industry—are moving to fill the need for specialized senior housing.

Companies in the hospitality industry such as Marriott and Hyatt, and health care organizations like National Medical Enterprises and Manor HealthCare Corporation have also entered the senior housing field. The results are a mixed bag, some genuine successes but many failures as well. Because of the high costs of development and the difficulties in measuring the size of the market and in judging the housing preferences of seniors, the field is not the surefire route to riches that many believe.

David B. Wolfe, an authority on senior markets and the past president of the National Association of Senior Living Industries, believes that the corporations from other fields that rushed into senior housing may be "deluded by the fool's gold of statistics." He says that most seniors make purchase decisions based on their desires distinct from their needs, and that marketing messages often fail to communicate in ways that are attractive to independent and active seniors who even though "by all reliable statistics, such discretionary prospects represent the vast majority of America's seniors, including those in the 75-64 cohort."

The major thrust of Wolfe's highly original and important theories is that *enhancement of life satisfaction* plays a major role in senior consumers' buying behavior and that successful marketing of discretionary products and services depends upon shaping the marketing strategy to satisfy this desire, but, "because projects are styled and offered primarily on the basis of need, rather than desire, mainly only those who 'need' a congregate environment are signing up."

He tells of watching the consumer behavior of an older couple at the supermarket where they have tied up the checkout counter with dozens of discount coupons on each of the carefully chosen items that relate to the coupons. After shopping they drive away in an expensive model

Mercedes. Wolfe contends that this couple personifies the consumer behavior of many affluent seniors—careful and thrifty about "need" purchases like food, but free spending to the point of extravagance when they perceive the purchase as an enhancement of life satisfaction, like an expensive, status automobile.

While his concepts are intended mostly for those involved in creating and marketing housing, his ideas are applicable to other industries as well.

Aging-In-Place

While it is true that vast numbers of older men and women have fled the harsh winters and crowded cities of the Northeast and Midwest to resettle in Florida, Arizona and other warm weather areas, the Census Bureau now confirms that most older men and women don't change their housing status until they are in their mid-70s or older. Arnold A. Goldstein, the Bureau's demographic researcher believes that most people want to stay where they are for as long as possible after retirement. Therefore, the housing market for seniors, as distinguished from the housing market for the general population, is based mostly with the elderly who move as a matter of need rather than preference.

An appreciation of the difference between a housing decision based on lifestyle preference versus a decision based on necessity can help marketers sharpen their approach and target their efforts to those who must move. Goldstein says that as one's personal mobility diminishes, especially among those of advanced age, "the dwelling of an older person becomes more and more that person's major environment. As health status changes and space needs diminish, the dwelling may become less suitable than it was at a younger stage of life. For example, stairs to bathrooms and bedrooms on upper floors may be difficult barriers. Yet moving to what would appear to be a more suitable residence may mean an upsetting change from a familiar neighborhood; from a physical setting imbued with years of memories; loss of privacy; a stressful confronting of

Retirees: When They Moved, Where They Moved

When They Moved ...

1 To 4 Years Before Retirement	15.4 percent
AT RETIREMENT	37.6
1 to 4 Years After Retirement	24.5
5 to 9 Years After	13.6
10 to 14 Years After	5.4
15+ Years After	3.7

Where They Moved ...

Different House	8.3 percent
Different Town	11.5
Different State	18.5
Did Not Move	61.6

Source: "Retired in America 1988m' a study by Retirement Advisors Division, Hearst Business Communications, New York.

new neighbors and possibly care givers; unfamiliar surroundings; and a new financial burden."

Home Modifications

As the number of households with elderly householders increases, planning to meet their housing needs and preferences could help those who wish to "age in place." Modifying
houses or apartments, to the changing health and mobility
capabilities of their residents, would allow people to remain
in their homes well into their later years. Limitations in
movement, strength, dexterity, eyesight or hearing, can
often be overcome by adding simple devises such as grab-
bars, kickplates and handlevers. Seniors who prefer to age
in place are in the market for devices and home modifications that will allow them to maintain their independence.

This list of companies currently manufacturing devices
used by older men and women to make it safer and easier
to live independently, is offered as an example of the opportunities open to companies interested in developing
products for the mature market . . .

Grab Bars prevent slipping, and helps user raise or lower
self to use bathroom appliances, counters, shelves, etc.
Manufactured by: Accessory Specialties, Inc., Yonkers, NY,
American Dispenser Company, Carlstadt, NJ, Franklin Brass
Manufacturing Co., Los Angeles, CA, JRD Enterprises, St.
Paul, MN, Maddak, Inc. Pequannock, NJ, KDI Paragon,
Pleasantville, NY., Tubular Specialties Manufacturing, Los
Angeles, CA.

Bathtub Seats are manufactured by Lunex, Inc., Bay Shore,
NY, Maddak Inc., Pequannock, NJ.

Portable Ramps provide access in home and buildings.
Manufactured by The Braun Corp., Winamac, IN, Copper-
loy, Independence OH, Handiramp, Inc., Mundelein, IL.

Automatic Door Operators   are manufactured by Besam, Inc. East Windsor, NJ, Overhead Door Corporation of Texas, Dallas, TX, Power Access Corporation, Collinsville, CT., Stanley Magic Door, Solon, OH, Keane Monroe Corp., Monroe, NC.

Sometimes the difficulties that older persons have in getting around their home cannot be resolved merely by adding a grab bar or new fixture, and extensive home remodeling is required. This creates business opportunities for building contractors who are familiar with the needs of seniors and the ways to make the necessary modifications practical and affordable. Many states and localities provide special grants and loans to their senior residents for such home remodeling.

CHAPTER TEN

MARKETING MEDICAL SERVICES

By the year 2000, health professionals can expect that three out of every four of all their care contacts will be with persons 65 and over. The logical consequence of the aging of America will have a tremendous impact on the medical and health care service industry as it struggles to meet the needs of a new generation of older health-care consumers.

The health care industry includes a vast array of service providers and product manufacturers. Among the service providers are doctors and dentists, hospitals, Health Maintenance Organizations (HMOs), clinics, medical centers, physical and mental therapists, chiropractors and fitness centers. Health care products include prescription drugs, over-the-counter medicines, vitamins and food supplements, eyeglasses, medical equipment for home use and a host of new self-testing and self-treatment devices that have recently appeared on the market.

The older men and women who represent the largest market for these products and services are knowledgeable self-reliant individuals whose top priority is good health. They are ready and able to try new products and services and take whatever steps are necessary to achieve their objective.

Health Care Spending

Although persons 65 and over represent only 12 percent of the population, they account for one-third of the nation's total personal health care expenditures.

Per capita spending for senior health reached $4,200 in 1984—an average growth rate of 13 percent per year from 1977 to 1984. Of the total amount spent for health care, older persons paid one-third through direct payment to providers or indirectly through premiums for insurance. In 1984, total personal health care expenditures for seniors were $120 billion.

Health Expenditures by Type for Younger and Older Urban Households

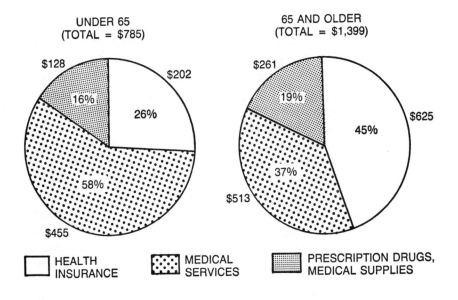

Note: Percentages may not equal 100 due to rounding.

Source: U.S. Bureau of Labor Statistics. Consumer Expenditure Survey: 1984 Interview Survey. Bulletin 2267, Washington: U.S. Department of Labor, August 1986.

Personal Health Care Expenditures for the Elderly By Source of Payment: 1984

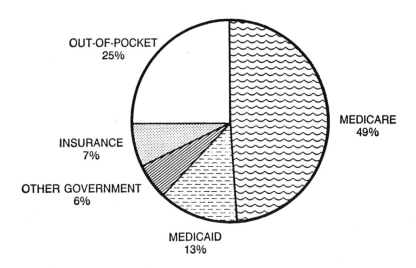

Source: Waldo, Daniel R. and Helen C. Lazenby. "Demographic Characteristics and Health Care Use and Expenditures by the Aged in the United States: 1977-1984." Health Care Financing Review Vol. 6, No. 1 (Fall 1984).

Medicare's major purpose is to finance acute health care services. In 1984, Medicare paid almost half of all personal health care expenditures for those covered.

Medicaid, a federal-state program, pays about 13 percent of the personal health care expenditure for the low-income elderly. Most of these payments are for the small percentage of the population that uses long-term care. Medicaid is the principal source of public financing for nursing home care. In 1985, it paid for 42 percent of all nursing home expenditures; consumers paid for another 51 percent through direct payments.

Where the Medicare Dollar for the Elderly Goes

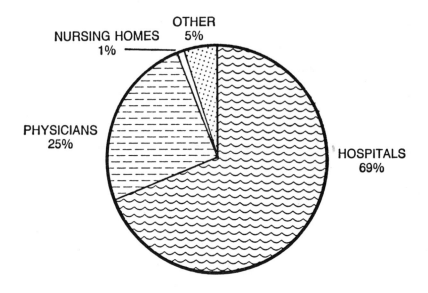

Source: Waldo, Daniel R. and Helen C. Lazenby. "Demographic Charac-
teristics and Health Care Use and Expenditures by the Aged in the
United States: 1977-1984." Health Care Financing Review Vol. 6,
No. 1 (Fall 1984).

Direct Costs for Consumers

Even though public funds provide a substantial part of their
health care costs, seniors bear considerable personal responsibility for health care.

In 1984, out-of-pockets health care expenses for seniors
averaged $1,059 per person. This does not include payments
for Part B/Medicare and for private health insurance. Most
of these expenses go for nursing home care, doctor visits
and health aids not covered by Medicare, Medicaid, or
private insurance.

The single greatest out-of-pocket liability for older Americans is for long-term care. Nursing home stays account for 80 percent of the expenses incurred by the elderly who have out-of-pocket costs over $2,000 per year. For those with out-of-pocket costs of less than $500 per year, 80 percent goes for prescription drugs and physician charges.

Many seniors who are not eligible for Medicaid purchase private supplemental health insurance, sometimes referred to as "Medigap," to protect themselves from the high out-of-pocket medical costs. The higher the income, the more likely the individual is to have private health insurance. Approximately 87 percent of seniors with incomes greater than $25,000 had Medigap coverage. In 1984, premiums for private supplemental insurance averaged about $300 to $400 per person. More recently the premiums were substantially higher, but the amount of the premium depends mostly on the extent of coverage, amount of deductible, etc.

Need for Marketing

Until recently, health services didn't think about such crass activities as "marketing"' That was something one did for breakfast cereals and automobiles. Why should medical services have to sell themselves to their public? The very idea was undignified, unethical and unnecessary.

These reasons were sound enough in the period from 1945 to 1975 when use of U.S. hospitals, physicians and other health services grew by an average of six percent each year, a record of growth that few industries could match. Since 1975, however, the growth rate has slowed and for some types of service and during particular periods the growth rate actually declined. Analysts consider one-quarter of all U.S. hospital beds surplus to need and, taking into account the large medical school enrollments, they project that by 1990 one doctor in every eight will be technically "unneeded." With the transition from shortage to surplus, consumers have more choices, and competition becomes a real factor for the industry. The stage is set for marketing, and the greater the competition, the more ag-

Supplementary Insurance Coverage by Medicare Enrollees

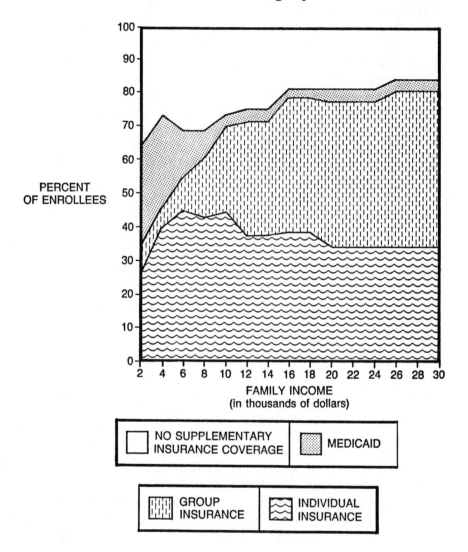

Note: People covered under both a group and an individual plan are likely
to have been classified above as covered by group insurance.

Source: Congressional Budget Office. Tabulations of 1984 Survey of Income and Program Participation (SIPP).

gressive the marketing. Seniors, the major consumers of health care services, have become a prime target of the industry's new marketing initiatives.

Insight to seniors' attitude to health care can help marketers to anticipate how they will respond to marketing strategies. A recent survey designed to get a better handle on the health care concerns of seniors, found that one-half of respondents age 55 and over perceived health care as an area of major concern; 85 percent said they visited a doctor at least once a year and more than half agreed that they "often think about how well their health care needs were being met." The survey conducted by Marketing Professors Elaine Sherman and Andrew M. Forman, for Hofstra University in New York, found 88 percent of those surveyed reporting that their health was as good or better than others their own age. Cost and physician empathy emerged as the two leading health care concerns of respondents of the Hofstra survey; 80 percent said that "they cared about having a doctor that really cared about his or her patients."

When asked about the usefulness of various information sources in regard to new health care products and services, the Hofstra survey found that interpersonal sources—advice from family and friend—were more important than mass media sources.

Sources of Information for Health Care Products and Services

Source	Percent of Subjects Mentioning as		
	Very Useful	Somewhat Useful	Of No Use
Personal doctor	66.4	27.4	6.2
Friends	24.5	59.6	15.8
Previous experience	40.4	42.1	13.9
Children	30.9	44.9	24.2
Spouse	42.9	27.4	29.8
Product Trials	15.2	49.0	38.7
Magazines	14.6	46.3	39.2
TV/Radio	13.2	43.0	43.8
Direct mail	10.4	32.3	57.2

Source: "What Do The Elderly Want And How Do They Select Health Care Services" by Elaine Sherman and Andrew M. Forman, Hofstra University, New York.

The Hofstra study and other research indicate that seniors are confident about their ability to make intelligent choices and that they they are informed about the benefits of new health care products and services. The marketing implications suggest that despite seniors' reliance on doctors, family and friends for information, advertising and other marketing activities played a part in laying the groundwork for "word of mouth." (For example, despite the obligatory putdown of direct mail as a source of information, it is likely that their doctor, whose advise they so esteem, received his information through the mail.)

One of the most frequent mistakes that health care marketers make is the assumption that seniors seek out medical service for physical and biological needs alone. Studies show that many people, but particularly seniors, who visit a doctor or clinic are more often satisfying psychological needs for reassurance and attention. Even through the visit may be medically useful, seniors will not derive the satisfaction they were seeking if they're treated mechanically and receive little or nothing in the way of psychological comfort. Whenever possible, this psychological reassurance factor should be built into the marketing message.

Marketers should also be aware of the importance of word of mouth in influencing older consumers—not just in health care but in all areas of consumer marketing. Strategies to stimulate word of mouth would include ads that suggest that you "tell your friends" and by making your advertising so interesting and informative that it provokes discussion and encourages seniors to "spread the word."

How Healthy Are They?

While most adults in their fifties and sixties are relatively healthy and not as limited in activity as generally assumed, the reality is that general health and a person's mobility decline with advancing age. Particularly in persons in their eighties and nineties, there's a greater likelihood of being limited in activity and the need for health services grows significantly.

Since the state of health depends in large measure on the individual's own perception of his or her condition, it is worth noting that, on average, older people have a positive view of their personal health. In a 1986 Health Interview Survey conducted by the National Center for Health Statistics, 70 percent of the seniors living in the community describe their health as excellent, very good or good compared with others their age. Only 30 percent of those surveyed report their health as fair or poor.

Since the survey does not include the institutionalized 65 and over population, the results may be positively biased. However, since marketers cater primarily to the older adults living in the community, the findings of the survey are a good indicator of the relevant target group.

An individual's perception of his or her personal health is often directly related to income. As the chart on page 206 indicates, about 24 percent of older persons with incomes over $20,000 described their health as excellent compared with others their age. Only 11 percent of those with low incomes reported excellent health.

The pattern of illness and disease has changed in the 20th century. Acute conditions were predominant among older people 80 years ago, but chronic conditions are now the more prevalent health problem. Although not necessarily limiting, chronic conditions are the burden of older age. Most visits to the hospital by older persons are for chronic conditions—arthritis, hypertensive disease, hearing impairments and, the most prevalent, heart disease.

Medical specialists expect substantial progress in the near future in reducing the severity of many of these chronic conditions. They point to increased control of hypertension, a major risk factor in heart disease, and such clinical innovations as renal dialysis and insulin pumps as examples of recent advances that could benefit older persons.

Data from a supplement to the National Health Interview Survey shows that one out of four of the 65 and over population had a health problem that caused difficulty with

Self-Assessment of Health by Income for Persons 65 Years and Older: 1986

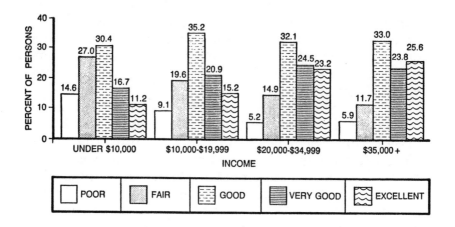

Source: National Center for Health Statistics. "Current Estimates from the National Health Interview Survey, United States, 1986." Vital and Health Statistics Series 10, No. 164 (October 1987).

one or more personal care activities, and about the same proportion had difficulty with at least one home management activity.

Since there is a greater prevalence of chronic conditions among seniors than there is in the general population, older men and women use medical personnel and facilities more frequently than their younger counterparts. On the average, persons 65 and older visit a doctor eight times a year (versus five visits by the general population). In addition, they are hospitalized twice as often as the younger population, stay 50 percent longer and use twice as many prescription drugs.

Hospital Use

Hospital use by seniors rose steadily between 1965 and 1983, but declined between 1983 and 1985. (Hospital use is measured by the number and rate of hospital discharges and by the average length of stay. While hospital "admissions" would seem to be a more logical way of measuring hospital use than "discharges," the government statistics used here are based on medicare charges that are calculated after discharge. (The American Hospital Association measures hospital use by admissions, but their statistics are not broken down by age.)

Physician's Services

Use of physician's services increases with age. In 1986, men and women age 45 to 64 averaged 6.6 doctor contacts a year, while those 65 and over averaged 9.1 doctor contacts.

The likelihood of seeing a doctor at least once during a given year increases somewhat with age. Among those in the 65 to 74 age category, 82 percent reported seeing a doctor during the last year versus 87 percent for those 75 or older. Since the enactment of Medicare, the average number of physician contacts, and the percentage of seniors that had seen a physician in the last year, have increased significantly.

The aging of the population will create a greater demand for physician care. The U.S. Administration on Aging projects that the demand for physician contacts will increase by 22 percent, from 250 million contracts to 305 by the end of the century.

Nursing Hones

Only about five percent of the elderly population are in nursing homes at any given time, but a greater percentage will live in nursing homes at some time during their lifetimes.

Interval Since Last Physician Visit

(Number in thousands)

	Less than 1 year	1 to 2 years	2 to 5 years	5 plus years
All ages	168,514	24,499	22,181	8,246
25 to 44	46,836	7,884	7,840	2,578
45 to 64	32,385	4,070	4,624	2,421
65 to 74	12,568	1,011	1,206	895
75 plus	8,070	449	558	367

Percent

	Less than 1 year	1 to 2 years	2 to 5 years	5 plus years
All ages	75.4	11.0	9.9	3.7
25 to 44	71.9	12.0	12.0	4.0
45 to 64	74.4	9.4	10.6	4.0
65 to 74	80.2	6.4	7.7	5.7
75 plus	85.4	4.8	5.9	3.9

Average Number of Visits per Person per Year

	Percent
All ages	5.2
25 to 44	4.8
45 to 64	6.1
65 to 74	7.4
75 plus	8.4

Source: America in Transition: *An Aging Society, 1984-85 Edition.* U.S. Senate Speical Committee on Aging.

In 1985, an estimated 1.3 million older individuals lived in nursing homes. An estimated one percent of the 65 to 74 year-old population were residents, compared to about six percent of those age 75 to 84 and about 22 percent of those 85 and over. The rate of nursing home use by seniors has almost doubled, from 2.5 percent to five percent, since the introduction of Medicare and Medicaid in 1966. The critical factor in the move to a nursing home is the absence of a spouse, child or other member of the family who can help provide the necessary care.

Given the growth of the elderly population, it is certain that the nursing home population will grow and the need for nursing home facilities and personnel will become critical. Projections show that between 1985 and the year 2000, the nursing home population will increase from 1.3 to 2 million.

Other Health Services

Use of health services other than hospitals, nursing homes, physician's services or informal care by a spouse or other caregiver, varies by type of service:

- Older persons visit dentists less often than the younger population. In 1986, only 43 percent of those over 65 had seen a dentist in the last year, compared with 59 percent for the general population.

- Seniors use more prescription drugs, vision aids, and medical equipment and supplies than younger segments of the population.

- Fifteen percent of seniors in 1980 were classified as "high users" of prescription medicine (25 or more prescriptions filled in the previous 12 months), compared to only two percent of those under 65.

- In 1979-80, 93 percent of older people had corrective lenses—eyeglasses or contact lenses—and 41 percent had one or more eye care visits in 1979.

- In 1985, 1.6 million Medicare beneficiaries received 39 million home health visits.

Pharmaceuticals

The longevity and general good health of today's older population is in large measure the result of major progress in the development of drugs. Developments in drug technology in the last half-century, have controlled or eradicated many debilitating and life-threatening diseases and added years to life. When today's seniors were born, fifty or more years ago, there were no antibiotics, no corticoids, few sulfa drugs, few vitamins, no tranquilizers, no antihypertensives, no antihistamines, no effective oral diabetic drugs, no prophylactic drugs for gout, no potent oral diuretics, no drugs to lower the level of blood lipids and cholesterol in the plasma. (V. Fuchs, *Who Shall Live?, Economics and Social Choice*, Basic Books, N.Y., 1974)

By the end of this century, major breakthroughs are expected in drugs to treat heart disease and stroke, two leading causes of death among the elderly.

The U.S. pharmaceutical industry markets two classes of drugs—prescription drugs which are obtained either from the medical practitioner or by a pharmacy, and nonprescription over-the-counter drugs which can be purchased without a prescription and are sold not only in drug stores, but in supermarkets and other retail outlets as well.

Prescription drugs are "a directed purchase"—that is, the sale of a prescription drug is not based on any choice of the consumer but rather that of the physician. Consequently, the physician is the target of prescription drug marketing. The sale of prescription drugs are promoted through personal visits to physicians by the drug manufacturer's sales representative and by direct mail and print advertising in medical journals.

Currently, seniors 65 and older take 400 million prescriptions per year. Despite the fact that older households have fewer members than their older counterparts, urban older adults spent twice as much—$261 versus $126—on prescription drugs and medical supplies. The National Council on Patient Information and Education estimates that by the end of this century, the 35 million older Americans in this age category will consume one-half of all prescription drugs. Consequently, these top ten U.S. pharmaceutical companies, manufacturers of prescription drugs, as well as over-the-counter medicines, will be among the major beneficiaries of the aging of America: Merk & Co, American Home Products, Pfizer, Eli Lilly, Bristol Myers,

Smithkline, Abbot, Warner-Lambert, Upjohn, Johnson & Johnson and Squibb.

In the context of this book, it should be noted that age bias can extend beyond the consumer and to the physicians who make drug purchase decisions. It has been reported that pharmaceutical advertisers frequently omit physicians over 65 year of age from their direct ail advertising based on the assumption that this group of physicians is less active in practice than their younger counterparts.

In his book, "Principles of Pharmaceutical Marketing," Professor Mickey C. Smith counsels drug marketers that age "cannot always predict the activity or importance of the physician. Patients, particularly the elderly, tend to continue going to the older physician with whom they have built up an accord over the years."

The Drugstore

"Our research with older consumers showed clearly that older adults respect pharmacists more than any other health professionals, considering them the most accessible members of the health care team. Many pharmacists have reported that paying attention to the special needs of older customers builds a large loyal clientele as well as contributing to the reduction of medication abuse."

This statement by Robert Bachman in a recent issue of "U.S. Pharmacist," may be difficult to apply to the giant drug chain that has replaced "Doc" Mitchell's corner drugstore, but staffing these stores with caring professionals who provide personal service is one of the best ways for the large chain operations to build a clientele of senior customers.

Over-The-Counter Medications

The over-the-counter drug industry began with the "patent medicine era" a hundred years ago. In the absence of professional standards and government regulation, such remedies were sold to a gullible public with extravagant claims and hints of a secret formula that would provide an instant cure for whatever ailed you.

Although some remnants of the patent medicine era remain in the way that a few non-prescription remedies are advertised today, for the most part they are a respectable and highly useful part of the health care universe. Self-medication with familiar drug products is an inexpensive and convenient way for older individuals to deal with simple health problems. Such drugs help to shield the medical professionals from a deluge of minor complaints. At a time of climbing health costs, self-medication helps to keep costs under control and lifts some of the burden from the nation's already burdened medical facilities.

Over-the-counter drugs for the self-treatment of common ailments such as headaches, muscle pains, heartburn, nasal congestion and other simple ailments are marketed primarily to the public and they can be purchased without a doctor's prescription. Self-medication with nonprescription medicines is the most prevalent form of medical care among older Americans. Older adults are heavy users of non prescription over-the-counter drugs; 70 percent of adults over 65 use some over-the-counter medication regularly. Self-treatment of everyday health problems with over-the-counter medicines is practiced by this age group at least 1.5 times every two weeks—nationally over a billion times each year.

The findings of a study by the Proprietary Association, a trade association for the over-the-counter drugs industry, reveal that older adults tend to be more likely to take some form of action than to ignore their health problems. Compared with adults 18-34, they are more likely to treat rather than tolerate perceived health problems. Adults over 65 used nonprescription medicines 35 percent of the time to take care of everyday health problems. Self-medication with nonprescription drugs serves as a screening mechanism which sorts out minor and self-treatable disorders from serious ailments requiring professional care.

The most common drug is this class is aspirin, which is used to treat the pain and inflammation associated with arthritis. Recent research suggests that one aspirin a day may help in averting heart attacks and many mature men and women are following this regimen. The categories of over-the-counter drugs most commonly used by older adults are . . .

Cough and cold remedies.

Pain killers.

Internal and external analgesics.

Antiacids and laxatives.

Foot preparations.

Eye lotions.

The importance of the 62 million Americans 50 and over to the pharmaceutical industry is reflected in Census Bureau statistics on the average *weekly* expenditures for non-prescription drugs and supplies by individuals in different age groups—from .85 a week for those under 25 to $4.39 for individuals 75 and over.

Age	Weekly Non-Prescription Expenditures
Under 25 years	$ .85
25-34	1.49
35-44	2.46
45-54	2.96
55-64	2.57
65-74	3.77
75 and over	4.39

The older segments of our population are the largest users of prescription drugs. While no comparable age-segregated statistics exist for non-prescription drugs, the U.S. Health Care Financing Administration reports total 1985 expenditures for drugs and sundries at more than $30 billion.

Increased technology and government review of over-the-counter medicines provides older consumers with a vast array of safe and effective medicines that they can purchase without a prescription. Many in the pharmaceutical industry see this as a "new era" of self-medication. This "new era" is fueled by the increased self-reliance and sophistication of our older population in health matters and by the increased willingness of the Food and Drug Administration to transfer established, safe prescription-only ingredients to over-the counter status.

Some 37 prescription-only drug ingredients have been recommended for transfer for direct consumer availability by independent scientists advising the FDA as part of an ongoing government review. More than one hundred over-the-counter medicines on the market today were available only by prescription seven years ago. A well-known example would be the prescription drug Motrin which recently became available for purchase without a prescription in brand names, Advil, Nuprin and Medipren or its generic name, "iboprophen."

Increased competition for a greater share of the market for established products, the need to promote a growing number of new products and a response to the public demand for more information about nonprescription drugs are the logical consequences of this "new era" of self-medication. The public demand for information is both an industry responsibility and a marketing opportunity. Speaking at a symposium sponsored by the FDA and The Proprietary Association, William L. Bergman, President of Richardson-Vicks USA, said that tomorrow's health care consumer will demand and industry must provide more and better information, and "good information begins with good labeling. But it doesn't end there. Advertising is a key part of the information process. It helps consumers to know what conditions are treatable and recommends appropriate medicines. It tells consumers to read and follow label directions. It is industry's obligation to use both labeling and advertising to ensure the flow of needed information to consumers."

Vitamins and Food Supplements

In addition to the nonprescription drugs that they take for minor ailments, many older Americans take vitamins, and nutritional supplements. Older women, for example, a group particularly susceptible to osteoporosis, take Calcium Supplements as a preventative.

Among the pharmaceutical giants positioned to benefit from the seniors' interest in vitamins are Warner-Lambert (Myadec), Miles Laboratories (One-A-Day Vitamins), Squibb (Theragram), American Cyanamid, Lederle and Schiff. Shaklee sells its products door-to door and other private-label vitamin manufacturers market by mail order or through health food retail stores. However marketed, vitamins and food supplements are an important part of the nutritional needs of older Americans.

How People Take Care of Everyday Health Problems

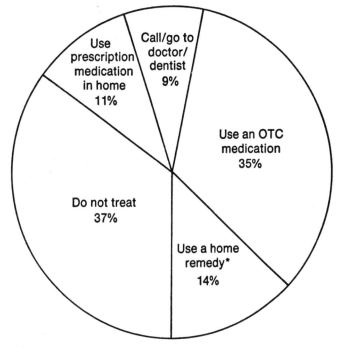

(Total adds to 106% because more than one action was taken in some cases.)

Note: Home remedies include salt-water gargles for sore throat and baking soda paste for bee stings—not medicines.

Source: From *Health Care Practices and Perceptions: A Consumer Survey of Self-Medication*, Harry Heller Research Corp.: 198.

HERE COME THE BABY BOOMERS

Any good duck hunter will tell you that the way to hit a target is to aim at where it's going to be, not at where it's been. The British call that "forward allowance." Good duck hunters that they are, marketers are setting their sights on a major target—the 75 million Americans born between 1946 and 1964. These are the baby boomers, a population segment that includes one in every three Americans.

There are more of them than the generation that came before and generation that follows. They are, in fact, members of the largest generation in U.S. history.

For many years now this baby boomer generation has been the darling of Madison Avenue, the gleam in the eye of every marketer with his eye on the prize. Well, the first of the baby boomers turn 50 in 1996 and four million or so will cross the threshold each year through 2004. What kind of consumers will they be? When they reach their seniority will they behave like the seniors that came before or will the special characteristics of their generation affect their consumer behavior in ways that we can begin to plan for now?

Because they were shaped by a completely different set of experiences and face a future greatly changed from the present, when the baby boomers become seniors their consumer behavior will be different than today's seniors. As a group, baby boomers as seniors will be even more diverse in health, wealth and lifestyle than current seniors. One can only look at where they're coming from and where they are now and try to make some educated guesses on the kind of consumers that the baby boomers will be in their later years. The term, "forward allowance" would be appropriate here.

In his book, *Baby Boomers*, Paul C. Light finds that despite their diversity, the baby boomers have much in common: "They grew up as the first standardized generation, drawn together by the history around them, the intimacy of television, and the crowding that came from the sheer onslaught of other baby boomers. They shared the great economic expectations of the 1950s and the fears that came with Sputnik and the dawn of the nuclear era. They shared the hopes of John F. Kennedy's New Frontier and Lyndon Johnsons's Great Society, and the disillusionment that came with the assassination, Vietnam, Watergate, and the resignations. To the extent these memories remain fresh, the baby boom will be a generation united."

When the the first of the baby boomers turn 50 in the mid-1900s, merchants with goods and services to sell can expect to find a large market made up of active and financially secure older adults—the best kind of customers. They will be the beneficiaries of many years of medical progress and general prosperity. They will have more years of life ahead and with the assets and pensions accumulated over a longer period of time, they will be able to enjoy the added years. In addition, they are more likely to have had a working spouse, thus enriching the nest egg and pensions.

Growing up in a relatively prosperous time, baby boomers could afford the luxury of seeking a meaningful philosophy of life and self fulfillment. The many options which opened up for them as a result of cultural change made relationships and responsibilities more difficult to handle but these are problems that are usually resolved with maturity.

The shortened work week, longer vacations and lifelong exposure to sports and recreation are preparing the baby boomers for retirement and make them good customers for recreation and travel, now and in the future. As seniors, they will be better educated and more interested in self-fulfillment and life satisfaction than the previous generation. The new seniors are more likely to be born and bred in urban rather than rural areas. Urban seniors have more options to live an individualistic lifestyle with more access to cultural facilities and better transportation. Having come from years of being "catered to," they will demand, and be in a position to afford, a variety of services designed to make life more comfortable. As children of the media age, the seniors of the future will be easier to reach with marketing communications.

Ready or not, here come the baby boomers—older, more conservative and, as a group, even more diverse than previous generations. The radicals of the 60s who became the "me generation" of the 70s and 80s will be the major component of the consumerist society of the 1990s. They represent a consumer market that is larger and more lucrative than any that came before. The extent to which you share in this dynamic mature market depends on the plans you make now.

ABOUT AARP

With a membership of 29 million and annual revenues of about $200 million, the American Association of Retired Persons (often referred to by its acronym, AARP), is the nation's largest private membership organization in the world. By way of comparison, the AFL-CIO has 15 million members. Of the 169 nations listed in the almanac, only 35 have populations larger than the AARP's membership. With its large, active membership comes power. Political power. Spending power.

This huge and influential organization was started quite modestly in 1958. Ethel Andrus, a retired high school principal, launched the organization from her home with meager resources and limited goals: She wanted to make it possible for people over 65 like herself to buy health insurance at an affordable price. While she saw it grow beyond her expectations, Ethel Andrus, who died in 1967, would be astounded if she were alive today and could see the huge and multi-faceted colossus that has grown from her little idea.

Modest dues (recently raised from $3 to $5 a year), aggressive marketing, extensive advertising and word-of-mouth extolling the discounts and member services, explain the flood of membership applications that pour into the organization's Washington, D.C. headquarters every day.

Despite its name, membership is open to all persons 50 years of age and over, whether retired or not. In fact, one of every four AARP members is still gainfully employed.

A subscription to the organization's official magazine *Modern Maturity* is, in itself, an important inducement to AARP membership. The popular bimonthly magazine boasts the largest circulation in the U.S., recently pushing ahead of circulation champions *TV Guide* and *Reader's Digest*. Advertisers spend about $27 million a year for advertising space in the *Modern Maturity*.

There are hundreds of private membership organization for seniors in the U.S., some with formidable membership rolls. The National Council of Senior Citizens with headquarters in Washington, D.C., has a membership of 4.5 million and 4,800 clubs across the nation. The National Alliance of Senior Citizens based in Arlington, Virginia has 2.2 million members. But the AARP with its 29 million members stands alone not only for the size of its membership and its rate of growth but for the political influence it wields and billions of dollars in purchasing power that it represents.

More than 3,700 local AARP chapters and 2,500 Retired Teacher Association units throughout the U.S. provide local support for the organizations aims and allow members to meet and socialize as they pursue their goals. While a paid staff of 1,300 run the organization—lobbying, conducting research, publishing material and implementing programs—more than 400,000 AARP volunteers keep things churning in the community. Their activities reflect the wide range of concerns of older Americans. They include criminal justice services, 55 Alive/Mature Driver Retraining, health advocacy, Lifetime Learning Institute, intergenerational and international activities and interreligious liaison, legal counsel for the elderly, a national gerontology information resource center, a tax aide program to assist in tax form preparation and a senior employment program to train and help place older men and women in permanent jobs.

A "nonpartisan" organization, AARP is nevertheless a major political force with strong advocacy positions and the voting power to convert its member's desires into law. Representing as it does almost 12 percent of the total U.S. population, it is widely acknowledged as the most influential lobby in the country, a force that no elected official or government employee can ignore. Together with 80 other national organizations, AARP is spearheading a drive to influence national and state legislation, expand medicare and provide long term care for the nation's older population. During the 1988 presidential election the organization spent over $8 million in TV spots and other advertising to "inform voters about issues of concern to older Americans."

Obviously, an organization involved in so many diverse areas and offering so much to so many is going to play a unique role in the lives of its members. Aside from its size and the political power that comes with large numbers organized for common purpose, what really makes the AARP unique is the way that it combines the traditional services of a not-for-profit membership organization with activities that compete head-on with commercial firms offering similar products and services. *Fortune* magazine says of AARP, "In large part it is a business itself, a golden-years nonprofit conglomerate." In that role, the AARP is a marketing machine, moving billions of dollars in merchandise and selling a wide variety of services to older Americans. If it was a public corporation, its $10 billion annual cash flow would place the AARP among the top 10 percent of the Fortune 500. Among the association's revenue-producing products and services are:

- Prescription medicines and other health care items sold by mail and by direct local purchase in retail pharmacies located in 12 major cities is a major source of revenue. AARP's mail order prescription service fills about seven million prescriptions a year.

- An investment program of seven mutual funds including income, growth and tax-free funds and a money fund, all managed by Scudder, Stevens and Clark.

- Supplemental health insurance (Medigap) to enable individuals 65 and over to supplement their government medicare benefits. From this one product alone, AARP takes in more than $50 million a year as the middleman for the six million members who buy health care insurance from Prudential Insurance company.

- A large number of escorted or independent travel packages and other domestic and international travel services at price tags from several hundreds of dollars for a 5 day trip to many thousands of dollars for a luxury cruise around the world.

- Motor Club memberships and automobile and homeowners insurance, a financial service offered by Hartford Insurance and sold to members by the AARP.

- A line of books co-published with Scott, Foresman and Company on subjects of interest to older readers.

According to Robert J. Forbes, an AARP director, these commercial activities are carried out by outside service firms that do not have the tax or cost advantages of nonprofit status. He says that the revenues that the Association receives from outside providers as "an administrative fee" goes into funding the large number of programs that the AARP is involved in for the benefit of all older Americans.

Learning From AARP

There are several aspects to the AARP phenomenon that commands the attention of business and of advertising and marketing professionals . . .

1. The growth of the AARP during its thirty year history parallels the growth of the mature population—in numbers, in its proportion to the rest of the population and in its impact on our society in general and the business community in particular. It is a measure of the size and depth of the mature market and the potential for even greater growth in the years ahead.

2. Shifts in the policy and the focus of activities at the AARP provide important clues to the changing interests of the nation's senior population. Health care insurance, the trend to generic drugs, consumerism and personal money management for older Americans are just some of the opportunities that were identified by AARP long before it was recognized by the business community.

   For example, in the early 1980s, when the banking industry placed a ceiling on the amount of interest that banks would pay savers, AARP started its own money market fund to provide members with a greater rate of return on their investments. Soon after, the bank ceilings were eliminated. In the meantime, the AARPs own investment program of mutual funds has grown to almost $3 billion in assets.

   Another example. In response to the increased costs of banking services and potential credit discrimination against older persons, the association has chartered its own Credit Union which according to the AARP "will offer competitive rates and services to give our members more financial options than ever before."

   The success that the organization has had in creating entities that offer these services provides valuable market research and inspiration for others seeking new windows of opportunity in the mature market.

3. The wide variety of subject matter in AARP publications provide valuable insight to the interests and concerns of the over-50 set. The publications range from free pamphlets and booklets to reasonably priced books on health, exercise, retirement planning, personal money management, travel and leisure. Some of the titles offer an unexpected view of the new and modern older generation and shatter some stereotype perceptions of later year lifestyles: *Divorce After 50, On the Road in a Recreational Vehicle, The Do-Able Renewable Home,* and *Home-Made Money—A Consumer's Guide to Home Equity Conversion.*

4. The AARP and the "outside providers" that carry on the commercial activities under an agreement with the association have become expert in marketing products and services to its mature membership. This expertise is the result of long experience in selling to a single age segment, and a special sensitivity to the needs and desires of older consumers. It is no surprise therefore that so many businessmen and women eager to tap the mature market, use AARP and its outsider providers as a marketing model. The future of the mature market, as viewed by standing on the shoulders of this marketing giant, is bright indeed.

5. The AARP has been a factor in influencing private enterprise to provide more and better options for older consumers. Control of the advertising accepted in its own magazine, *Modern Maturity*, gives the association the clout to impose standards on the way that the advertising message is conveyed. The association has been using its influence with industry leaders and with advertising and marketing firms to spread a positive message about aging in America.

The AARPs biennial convention, the most recent held in Detroit in 1988 and attended by 30,000 embers, provides insight to the diversity of senior interests in our senior population and the potential that these interests represent for business. Concurrent sessions during the three-day conference in the motor city's huge Cobo Conference/Exhibition Center featured an impressive line-up of celebrated "experts." At one point, attendees at the convention had to make the hard choice between Ralph Nader ("The only real aging is the aging of one's ideas") and Dr. Ruth Westheimer, the sixty year old sexologist whose explicit sex talk is so popular that she was invited back by popular demand after her appearance at the previous convention. In a tongue-in-cheek account of the conference in *The New Yorker*, E.J. Kahn, Jr. observed that Nader attracted more men than women, Dr. Ruth more women than men. From this fact you are free to draw your own conclusions.

Other prominent speakers at the convention included columnist Art Buchwald, TV's Wall Street Week host Louis Rukeyser, chef Craig Claiborne, TV medical commentator Dr. Art Ulene, Dear Abby (Abigail Van Buren), U.S. Senator Donald Riegle and Robert Ball, the former U.S. Commissioner of Social Security.

At a separate Exhibit Hall, roughly the size of the football field, over a hundred exhibitors, offered a wide range of goods and services to the mature attendees of the conference. The list of exhibitors at the Detroit conference reads as a kind of "Who's Who" in the forefront of marketing to the mature consumer. To give you an idea of the kinds of companies getting ready to tap the mature market, here are some of the 133 exhibitors at the last AARP convention . . .

Air India / ALCAS Cutlery / American Express/ AMTRAK / AT&T / Bi-Folkal Productions / British Tourist Agency / Campbell Soups / Charm Step Shoe Co. / Colony Hotels and Resorts / Denny Restaurants / Doubleday Large Print Home Library / Franklin Computer / Fuller-Brush/ Gray Line Sight Seeing / Grosse Pointe Moving & Storage/ Hertz Corporation / Hot Springs Convention & Visitors Bureau / Howard Johnson Hotels & Lodges / Kelly Services/ McDonald's / National Bowling Council / New Zealand Tourist Office / Omni Hotels / Rockport Shoe Co / Sanka Coffee (General Foods) / Thompson Worldwide Recreational Vehicles/ Time Inc. / United Airlines / Universal Gym Equipment/ World Wide Games . . . *and 103 others.*

APPENDIX C
RESOURCES

"Knowledge is of two kinds. We know a subject ourselves, or we know where we can find information about it."

Since Samuel Johnson made that statement two centuries ago our body of knowledge has expanded beyond measure but the validity of his statement still holds.

A cottage industry of researchers, consultants, associations and specialists is emerging to provide knowledge and information about a market of increasing importance to U.S. industry. This increased attention comes in recognition of the large number and spending power of older Americans and in anticipation of the greater importance of this segment of the population in the 1990s.

Collectively and individually, these resources provide marketers with a variety of support services and with statistics and insight to the various age categories within the mature market. Some serve as a clearing house for the exchange of relevant information and ideas on this specialized field of marketing.

Both government and private organizations provide valuable research relating to older consumers in the U.S. For the conscientious searcher, there is information everywhere—sometimes in places that you would least expect it. In the pages that follow we list some of the organizations that offer useful research and services on the

229

subject. There is space here for only brief comment on each listing. Obviously, there is much more in the way of information and help that these sources can provide. Each of these organizations will respond to your inquiry should you wish to inquire further about their activities and publications.

Since new studies and information on the subject is constantly being developed, the reader is urged to explore the territory with a fresh eye and seek out current data most applicable to specific marketing problems.

Research and Services

Goldring & Co, Inc.
820 North Orleans
Chicago, IL 60610
312 440-5252

Known for its research and "The Geromarket Study" of 50+ consumers. The seven volume study provides data on six market segments with each group's preferences for a range of products and services.

Simmons Custom Studies
380 Madison Avenue
New York, NY 10017
212 916-2300

Produced a 200-page study, "The Golden Generation: Age 50+ Market." The study provides information on eight key groups with survey data on a variety of products and services. Simmons also does custom studies.

Howard Marlboro Group
475 Tenth Avenue
New York, NY 10018
212 736-2300

Research entitled "The Swing Generation." Provides custom research and marketing services.

Frost & Sullivan Inc.
106 Fulton Street
New York, NY 10038
212 233-1080

Research entitled "Geriatric Strategy Opportunities for Personal and Health Care Products."

Age Wave Inc.
1900 Powell Street, Suite 800
Emeryville, CA 94608
415 652-9099

Research entitled "Marketing Healthcare to Older Adults."

Impact Resources
779 Brookedge Blvd.
Columbus, OH 43081
614 899-1563

Operates MA*RT USA, a computerized database with special segment on 65+ age group. Published hardcopy research report, "Seniors."

Daniel Yankelovich Group
1350 Sixth Avenue
New York, NY 10019
212 247-1313

This well-known research organization has produced "The Mature Americans: A Study of Today's Men and Women 50 Years and Over" and other studies on older consumers, mostly in conjunction with and on assignment for organizations and media.

CACI, Inc.
Market Analysis Division
3040 Williams Drive
Fairfax, VA 22031
800 292-2224
703 698-4600

Produced the "55+ Report." Provides custom demographic reports for marketers.

Claritis
201 N. Union Street
Alexandria, VA 22314
703 683-8300

Operates several cluster systems, among them: PRIZM, classifies U.S. households into 40 neighborhood types. P$YCLE, a cluster system for financial services which provides data on income, age, etc.

Generation Marketing, Inc.
1 Lincoln Plaza
New York, NY 10023-7177
212 496-9280

This firm's database, Agebase, contains the names and addresses of over 175,000 individuals by age (exact date of birth) and income. It is enhanced with other indicators which allows marketers to identify lifestyle as well as demographics.

Cambridge Reports Trends & Forecasts
675 Massachusetts Avenue
Cambridge, MA 02139
617 661-0110

Among its research reports are "Retirement, Health and Insurance: Issues for an Aging Population" and "Consumer Planning and Preparation for Retirement."

The 35+ Committee
Marketing Center, Suite 1700
675 Third Avenue
New York, NY 10017
212 818-9060

An organization that studies radio listening patterns of mature consumers and the effectiveness of radio advertising on this segment of the population.

Consumer Research Center
The Conference Board
845 Third Avenue
New York, NY
212 759 0900

This prestigious research organization produced a research study "Midlife and Beyond" (sponsored by CBS) and other data on older consumers.

Center for Social Research in Aging
University of Miami
Coral Gables, FL 33124
305 264-4114

Published an innovative study on "The Economically Advantaged Retiree: State Statistical Profiles."

Phoenix Systems, Inc.
525 West 22d Street
Sioux Falls, SD 57105
605 339-3221

Phoenix is a marketing research, promotion and training firm that serves companies offering products and services to older consumers.

Business Forum on Aging
The American Society on Aging
833 Market Street, Suite 516
San Francisco, CA 94103
415 543-2617

Helps firms with issues involving aging, including marketing. For an annual fee corporate members receive publications, attend conferences and network on relevant matters.

LifeSpan Communications
51 East 90th Street
New York, NY 10128
212 678-0913

This research and marketing company specializes in the 50+ markets.

Wolfe Resources
209 West Street
Annapolis, MD 21401
703 758-0759

Originators of the "Life Satisfaction" theory of senior consumer behavior.

Center for Mature Consumer Studies
Georgia State University
University Plaza
Atlanta, GA 30303-3083
404 651-4177

Professor George Moschis, director of the Center, has produced a major study, "Consumer Behavior of Older Adults: A National View."

U.S. Travel Data Center
1899 L Street NW
Washington, D.C. 20036
202 293-1040

Involved in extensive research on senior travel and vacation patterns.

The Markle Foundation
75 Rockefeller plaza
New York, NY 10019
212 489-6655

Published "Pioneers on the Frontier of Life: Aging in America" conducted by the Daniel Yankelovich Group.

Advanced Living Systems Division
Institute for Technology Development
428 N. Lamar Blvd.
Oxford, MS 38655
601 234-0158

This is a research and development team that seeks solutions to meet the needs of an aging population. The team addresses problems created by products and environments.

Judith Langer Associates Inc.
301 E. 87th Street
New York, NY 10028
212 348-0684

Produced a lifestyle study of 50+ consumers.

American Health Care Association
1201 L Street NW
Washington, D.C. 20005
202 842-4444

Association of health care suppliers. Publishes *Provider* magazines. Conducts research on design and product specification for housing and manufacturing industries that cater to seniors.

Donnelley Marketing
70 Seaview Avenue
Stamford, CT 06904
203 353 7429

Conducted survey, "New Age: Perspectives On The Over 50 Market"

MRCA Information Services
2215 Sanders Road
Northbrook, IL 60062
312 480-9600

This company creates "Menu Census" studies on food preferences of older Americans.

PrimeLife Marketing Division
The Data Group Inc./IRI
Meetinghouse Business Center
2260 Butler Pike, Suite 150
Plymouth Meeting, PA 19462
215 834-2080

This division of a large research company offers mature market-related consultation, research and training.

National Gerontological Resource Center AARP
1909 K Street NW
Washington, D.C. 20049

Probably the largest library and clearing house of information about older Americans.

AgeLine Database
BRS Information Technologies
1200 Route 7
Latham, NY 12110
800 345-4BRS
518 783-1161

A computerized database accessed by commuter network subscribers provides reference on chosen topic in minutes. Indexed by 1,700 subject terms, contains abstracts for 20,000 documents on aging.

Professional Associations

National Association for Senior Living Industries
184 Duke of Gloucester Street
Annapolis, MD 21401
301 263-0991

A coalition of aging associations, health care providers, and over 600 corporate purveyors of products and services. Publishes *Spectrum*, a magazine for industries serving seniors. Recently commissioned and published a study by SRI International on "Lifestyles and Values of Older Adults" (LOVOA).

Mature Market Institute
20 Chevy Chase Circle
Washington, D.C. 20015
202 363-9644

An association of companies and individuals involved in marketing to older consumers. Holds seminars and publishes a newsletter for members.

National Council on the Aging Inc.
600 Maryland Avenue SW
Washington, D.C. 20024
202 479-1200

NCOA is a resource for information, technical assistance and research on every aspect of aging.

American Society on Aging
833 Market Street, Suite 512
San Francisco, CA 94103
800 537-9728
415 543-2617

Professional organization for gerontologists.

American Marketing Association
250 South Wacker Drive
Chicago, IL 60606-5819
312 648-0536

The library of this national organization maintains an extensive file on the mature market.

Membership Organizations

American Association of Retired Persons
1909 K Street NW
Washington, D.C. 20049
202 728-4300

Very large, very influential, aggressive marketers. Twenty nine million members 50 and over. See Appendix B, "About AARP."

National Council of Senior Citizens
925 15th Street NW
Washington, D.C. 20005
202 347-8800

A private membership organization with 4.5 million members

National Alliance of Senior Citizens
2525 Wilson Blvd.
Arlington, VA
703 528-4380

There are 2.2 million members of the Alliance.

Gray Panthers Project Fund Inc.
311 S. Juniper Street, Suite 601
Philadelphia, PA 19107
215 545-6555

Over 80,000 members, 80 networks in 30 states.

National Association of Area Agencies on Aging
600 Maryland Avenue SW, Suite 208
Washington, D.C. 20024
202 484-7520

This agency offers data on product and service needs of seniors. It offers opportunities for joint ventures in senior-oriented enterprise.

SeniorNet
University of San Francisco
San Francisco, CA 94117-1080
415 666-6505

Operates a computer network for individuals 55 and over and local, organization-sponsored computer equipped sites in the U.S. and Canada. Also holds conferences and conducts research on use of computers by seniors.

Newsletters For Marketing Professionals

"Mature Market Report"
Lifestyle Change Marketing
455 East Paces Ferry Road, Suite 332
Atlanta, GA 30305
404 264-1404

Editorial offices:
801 E. Campbell, Suite 110
Richardson, TX 75081

A monthly newsletter, subscription rate is $147 per year.

"Selling to Seniors"
CD Publications
8555 16th Street. Suite 100
Silver Spring, MD 20910
301 588-6380

A monthly newsletter, subscription rate is $127 per year.

"Maturity Market Perspectives"
Wolfe Resources Group
209 West Street, Suite 201
Annapolis, MD 29401
301 268-0370

A bi-monthly newsletter, subscription rate is $60 per year.

"Senior Market Report"
244 West 54th Street, Suite 706
New York, NY 10019
212 974-3279

This new monthly newsletter is available at a subscription fee of $225 per month.

Government Research Sources

Several government agencies collect, tabulate and publish a wide range of statistical data profiling the older population.

U.S. Department of Commerce
Bureau of the Census
Suitland, MD 20233
301 763-7883

U.S. Administration on Aging
Office of Management and Policy
330 Independence Avenue SW
Washington, D.C. 20201
202 245-0641

U.S. Travel and Tourism Administration
Department of Commerce
Washington, D.C. 20230
202 377-0136

National Center for Health Statistics
3700 East-West Highway
Hyattsville, MD 20782
301 436-8500

U.S. Department of Labor
Bureau of Labor Statistics
Division of Consumer Expenditure Surveys
Bicentennial Building
600 E Street, NW
Washington, D.C. 20212
202 272-5156

U.S. Office of Consumer Affairs
1009 Primer Building
Washington, D.C. 20202
202 634-4319

Congressional Committees:

House Select Committee on Aging
House Annex #1
Washington, D.C. 20515
202 224-5364

Senate Special Committee on Aging
Hart Senate Office Building, Room 628
Washington, D.C. 20510
202 224-5364

Marketing and Research Associations

American Marketing Association
250 South Wacker Drive, Suite 200
Chicago, IL 60606
312 648-0536

This professional society of marketing executives publishes a directory of members and several trade journals and magazines.

Marketing Research Association, Inc.
111 East Wacker Drive, Suite 600
Chicago, IL 60601
312 644 6610

This is a national association of market research professionals. They publish trade journals and an annual industry sourcebook.

Industry Sources of Data, Research and Information on Older Adult Consumers

American Bankers Association, 90 Park Avenue, New York, NY 10016

American Booksellers Association, 175 Fifth Avenue, New York, NY 10010

American Carpet Institute, 350 Fifth Avenue, New York, NY 10001

American Council of Life Insurance, 1850 K Street, Washington, DC 20006-2284

American Meat Institute, 59 East Van Buren Street, Chicago, IL 60605

Bowling Proprietors' Assoc. of America, West Higgins Rd, Hoffman Estates, IL 60172

Florists' Telegraph Delivery Assoc., 900 W. Lafayette Boulevard, Detroit, MI 48226

Food Marketing Institute, 1750 K Street NW, Washington, D.C. 20006

The Proprietary Association, 1150 Connecticut Ave., NW, Washington, D.C. 20036

Menswear Retailers of America, 390 National Press Building, Washington, D.C. 20004

National Appliance and Radio-TV Dealers Association, 1329 Merchandise Mart, Chicago, IL 60654

National Association of Food Chains, 1725 Eye Street, NW, Washington, D.C. 20006

National Association of Retail Grocers of the United States, 360 N. Michigan Avenue, Chicago, IL 60601

National Home Furnishing Association, 1150 Merchandise Mart, Chicago, IL 60654

National Restaurant Association, 1530 North Lake Shore Drive, Chicago, IL 60610

National Retail Merchants Association, 100 West 31st Street, New York, NY 10016

National Sporting Goods Association, 23 East Jackson Boulevard, Chicago, IL 60604

Super Market Institute Inc. 200 East Ontario St., Chicago, IL 60611

United Fresh Fruit and Vegetable Association, 777 14th Street, Washington, D.C. 20005

Suggested Reading

Marketers who wish to learn more about the mature market will find a wealth of material in libraries and research facilities across the nation. In addition, there is a continuous flow of new books publications to help interested professionals keep abreast of new developments in this evolving and constantly changing marketplace.

In the meantime, here is suggested reading list, a "starter set" of publications which in themselves provide a well-rounded introduction to the world of the older consumer in America.

Books

"Lifestyles and Consumer Behavior of Older Americans," by Howard G. Schutz, Pamela C. Baird and Glenn R. Hawkes. Published by Praeger, a division of Holt, Rinehart and Winston.

"Aging America," prepared by the staff of the U.S. Senate Special Committee on Aging, printed and distributed by the U.S. Department of Health and Human Services.

"The Facts on Aging Quiz," by Erdman B. Palmore. Springer Publishing

"Statistical Handbook on Aging Americans" edited by Frank L. Schick. Oryx Press.

"Our Aging Society, Paradox and Promise." edited by Alan Pifer and Lydia Bronte. Published by W.W. Norton & Co.

"TV's Image of the Elderly," by Richard and James Davis. Lexington Books.

"Advertising Health Services," by Trevor A. Fisk. Pluribus Press.

"Why They Buy" by Robert B. Settle and Pamela L. Alreck. John Wiley & Sons, Inc.

"The Economically-Advantaged Retiree" by Charles E. Longing, Jr. and Steven G. Ullman. Published by the Center for Social Research in Aging, Coral Gables, Florida.

"Age Wave" by Ken Dychwald and Joe Flower. Published by Jeremy P. Tarcher Inc., distributed by St. Martins Press.

Booklets and Pamphlets

"Pioneers on the Frontier of Life: Aging in America," published by The Markle Foundation.

"Midlife and Beyond," prepared by the Conference Board and sponsored by CBS/Broadcast Group.

"The Mature Americans," a publication of the American Association of Retired Persons.

"The Economic Impact of Older Adults," a publication of Life Options Program, Little Rock, Arkansas.

"American Demographics" magazine frequently publishes articles on the 50+ market. Reprints are available from American Demographics, P.O. Box 68, Ithica, NY 14851. Phone: (800) 828-1133.

An Honor Role Of Senior Ads

The mature market would appear to be Madison Avenue's blind spot. Even though there is currently more of it than there was just a few years ago, good advertising targeted to older consumers is not easy to find. The formidable buying power of the older adult population is not being as effectively tapped through advertising as it could be.

There are several reasons for such missed opportunities. The creator of advertising for this market walks a careful line between "straight talk" and offending the sensibilities of his mature prospect. While so much advertising to this market is for products and services that alleviate the problems of aging, the advertising professional must find creative ways to convey a positive message. The ad must be specific enough to attract the attention of the senior without direct reference to age—a major turn off among older consumers.

In addition, advertisers fear "age-typing" their product or service and losing their younger markets in the process. The relative youth of most of the men and women who create the advertising is another explanation for the dearth of good advertising for senior markets. From their vantage point, seniors are sedentary, frugal, and closed to new concepts and ideas. They portray older people in their ads as sickly and foolish.

Even though there is mounting evidence that none of these negative images are valid, the stigma persists and ads continue to appear which invoke outdated and offensive stereotypes of seniors.

Fortunately, enough advertisers have found a way to shape their message and create upbeat, effective advertising that gets results. They serve as a model for other advertisers eager to tap the mature market. While the examples that follow represent a wide range of products and services they all display the sensitivity to the needs, desires and consumer that makes for successful advertising. The ads are designed to attract the attention of mature adults but at the same time avoid the stereotyped approach that has characterized such advertising in the past. They reflect a recognition of the new generation of seniors—healthier, more active and more free spending than any generation of seniors that came before.

For example . . .

Lodging, Hotels, Travel

"50% Off Is Nothing to Snooze At." (Illustration: A smiling TV Weatherman Willard Scott lying in bed.)

A Howard Johnson Hotels and Motor Lodges ad announcing 50 percent discount for adults 60 and over. The ad combines two elements important to seniors. First, the importance of discounts to older travelers and second, the endorsement of a credible personality who helps the reader "find himself" in the ad. Willard Scott, a jovial regular on the NBC Today show, announces the birthdays of centenarians and has a following among seniors.

"Dependable lodging on a retirement budget."

Without mentioning a specific age—something older adults are said to resent—Best Western Hotels, Motor Inns and Resorts has zeroed in on its target. The word "retirement" helps mature people know that this ad is speaking to them, whether they are retired or not. "Dependable" and "budget," are no-nonsense words which speak to no-nonsense seniors on the move

"Another cliche bites the dust." (Illustration: Rocking Chair and Slippers.)

Continental Airlines used this headline and illustration to announce its Golden Travelers Passport, which allows passengers 62 and over a certain number of round trips per year at a highly favorable one-time payment. The copy says, "Continental is retiring a lot of preconceived notions about discount travel programs." The claim is justified because the cost per trip is lower than any discounted fare.

"Holiday Inn Salutes America's Golden Medalists."

The photograph shows runners in the National Senior Olympic Games. The copy announces its sponsorship of the event and says, "At Holiday Inn we've established a track record of our own based on comfort and dependable service," thus catering to the highest priorities of older travelers.

"Now that you're older you know how to plan a better trip."

This United Airlines ad for its Silver Wings Plus program of discounts for adults 60 and over is a prime example of creativity and sensitivity applied to mature market advertising.

The illustration: A browned-out photo of a four-year old on a pony—it evokes instant recognition, a smile and a memeory. Every senior has a photo like this somewhere in the attic.

The copy starts: "You were going to ride the range and explore new frontiers. But before you knew it, responsibilities trotted in and your dreams were corralled. Now United Airlines has made it easier to hit the trail . . ."

A mail solicitation from Michael Reese HMO Senior Plan in Chicago shows an old photograph of a returning World War II GI kissing his girl friend. The headline reads . . .

"Remember when health care cost was the last thing on your mind?"

Here is nostaligia with a point to make. The famous photograph combined with a clever headline says: We know you and we have something to tell you about a subject that is important to you *now*. This direct mail advertisement, sensitive to most senior's reticence about being labelled, identifies the need for an age-related service without once mentioning age. A neat trick, neatly executed.

Automobiles

"Now you can comfortably afford to live in the lap of luxury."

This ad for Chevrolet Classic Brougham shows that GM marketers have read the studies on the qualities that older Americans look for in their automobile. Comfort, luxury and affordability—the three hot buttons for the senior car buyer.

"Seville. With an exclusive V8 and elegant new interior, it gives equal time to performance and comfort."

Whoever decided to advertise the high-priced, top-of-the-line Cadillac automobile in a senior magazine knows where his bread is buttered. Older Americans have the taste and the pocketbook that goes with this well established brand-name. The senior set prefers American cars over the imports, and Cadillac is wise to keep their best customers from straying.

If there was a Hall of Fame for mature market advertising, the prime candidate for honors would have to be the Ford automobile ad.

A large double-spread four color ad in Modern Maturity magazine shows a sleek, seductively glamorous convertible automobile—a white Ford Escort with the top down. Beneath the photo just one line of copy:

"Just when the kids thought they had you all figured out."

No further comment is necessary. Like all good advertising it speaks for itself. The ad was created by the Detroit office of J. Walter Thompson advertising agency.

Food

"More With Less."

Campbell Soups promotes its Special Request line of soups (with one-third less salt) in senior magazines and in general magazines with a large proportion of older adult readers as well as in television commercials magazines adjacent to shows which attract large numbers of older viewers. Many people over 50 are concerned about high blood pressure and when their doctor says, "Cut down on salt," they listen. Campbell Soups listens too.

"Lena Horne on getting the best out of life—'Taking care of my voice, body, and taste buds is what keeps the brass in the horn.'"

The photograph that accompanies this headline says it all. A genuine beauty at age 72, Lena Horne is the perfect spokesman for Post Bran Flakes. Most consumers know that bran is healthy so the ad people are wise to emphasize that it's also good for the "taste buds."

"A Nutritious Dinner . . . Not Just Another Fish Story." (Illustration: Bowl of bran flakes and strawberries.)

Addressing the older adults interest in nutrition, this ad for Kellogs Bran Flakes, is copy heavy but full of the kind of information that interests seniors. It contains a detailed comparison of the nutritional value of a bowl of flakes, fruit and milk versus a broiled flounder dinner; nutritionally speaking, the flakes come out looking good. This ad is also an interesting attempt to promote a traditional breakfast food for other meals throughout the day.

"Caution: Think Twice Before You Eat This Salad." (Illustration: Salad greens with an unlabeled bottle of salad dressing.)

This ad for Good Seasons salad dressing mix in an envelope reminds readers that bottled salad dressing contains a large amount of oil with saturated fat—"you mix Good Seasons dressing yourself. So you can choose an oil lower in saturated fat." Seniors trying to lower cholesterol intake are seeking ways to do so and authoritative diet information gets high readership.

Two McDonalds TV commercials have won the hearts of seniors and the accolades of marketers. The first, "The New Kid," portrays an older gentleman in his first day on the job at a McDonalds restaurant. He pleases the customers and makes friends with younger workers who benefit from his instruction. This commercial, which was honored as one of the five favorite commercials of '87, not only built goodwill for McDonalds but helped the company with a major problem—recruiting older men and women to alleviate the need for competent help.

One third of McDonald's customers are older adults. Another commercial for the fast-food chain features latter-year romance. An older gentleman approaches a mature women sitting alone at a table. He timidly inquires whether the seat is taken. She smiles, says it isn't, he joins her. Is this the beginning of a relationship?

Perhaps the reason for the success of these two outstanding commercials is that they portray situations that defy the stereotype. In the first one, an older man is shown happily and productively at a job usually associated with young people. The second, the potential for mature romance where you'd least expect it.

"Go ahead, Grandma. It won't bite.'"

The photo shows a ten-year old boy and his silver-haired grandmother sitting on the porch steps enjoying a pitcher of Minute Maid Reduced Acid Orange Juice. The copy reads: "It's a gentler orange juice. Gentler, because we found a way to remove a lot of the acid, yet still keep the juice 100% pure and delicious."

Housing

"Lucille, True and Dorothy would like to tell you a thing or two about The Village at Forest Glen. Over lunch."

This headline in an ad for a Beavertown, Oregon housing development is an invitation to lunch or dinner on the house and a chance to meet current residents. The three residents mentioned in the headline are pictured in the ad and residents give the tour so prospects are not subjected to a "hard sell." Ads in the real estate section of local newspapers are supplemented with radio spots.

"Retirement Plans For Those Who Refuse To Retire."

The illustration for this ad for GHM housing shows a schematic drawing of a modern apartment. The copy starts with the question: "Do you envision retirement as the most active, exciting and rewarding time of life? A time for real choices. If so, you should know more about GHM." The ad lists and describes its various housing developments in several states. It offers a choice in design, lifestyle and home ownership, "combined with the security of a state of the art health insurance and health care programs."

This ad which appeared in the first issue of the *New York Times* Sunday Supplement "The Best Years," addresses the desires of seniors to remain active and their concerns about security and health care. The ad shows a real understanding of the psyche of today's older American.

"We give you time when you're 'not ready yet'."

Marketing housing to seniors is mostly a matter of timing. Many seniors are interested in the facilities and lifestyle offered by senior housing but they'll tell you, "I'm not ready yet." An ad in "Golden Years" magazine for Lakeview Terrace, a community still under construction, acknowledges this fact and tells the reader, "We think we have the answer for those of you who are 'not ready yet' for a senior living community. We aren't quite ready either."

The ad turns procrastination into an advantage; while the project is under construction prospects have a wide choice of apartment design and can actually customize an apartment to match their needs and preference.

"Classic Residence by Hyatt. People who get into it are always getting out."

Hyatt, the hotel people, are active in senior housing developments and their ads for housing developments in New Jersey, Maryland and Texas speak to seniors interested in the benefits of special housing without being "ghettoized"—"a unique rental community for seniors who want the freedom to get out and enjoy themselves. Whether it's a shopping trip, dinner and a show, or just a walk through the neighborhood."

"Go For It!"

Beverly Hills Retirement Housing is fighting the image of retirement housing as a place for passive old people. By using the battle cry of the pleasure seeker they are saying a lot in a few words.

Financial Services

"Nuveen. It's the investment of certainty in a climate of uncertainty."

Nuveen Unit Trust advertises "steady tax-free interest that assures you you'll keep the money you earn" and tells readers that the fund is "one of the closest things to a sure thing you can find." It also reminds readers that it is insured by MBIA, a comfort to people who are at that stage of life where safety is the first and most important thing they seek in an invetsment. The conservative, reassuring approach in this ad is a direct response to the insecurities of older adults concerning money and investments.

"At 62, Donald Henness discovers a sculpture in each piece of wood and an opportunity in a variable annuity from the Prudential." (Illustration: Sculptor Henness in his workshop carving a large block of wood.)

While many specialists in the field warn against ads which are age-specific, this ad warrants an exception. Insurance is one of those products that are age-specific and the best way to handle it is to address it head on. This ad for Prudential softens its blatant mention of age, by showing an active older man engaged in a vigorous activity. It also benefits from the unstated but effective connection between the solidity of wood and its "solid" annuity program.

"We counselled him on estate planning, his son on tax matters and taught his granddaughter about zero-coupon bonds." (Illustration: Mature man and family about to ascend in a hot air ballon.)

This adventurous and obviously affluent family is a model for the kind of customer that U.S. Trust is looking for in its ad. The financial firm talks about its "Uncommon expertise in managing wealth" and offers well-heeled seniors "multi-generational financial counselling."

Beauty Care

"JOURNEY for the special woman who dares to be herself. Defines her own passions. And, whatever her age, sees life as a journey to grow, achieve, emerge." (Illustration: Middle aged female model.)

All that in a perfume? Oh well, perfume advertising is allowed some poetic license. The point is that Esse Perfumes has created a perfume to suit the fragarance preferences of older women and is using the ad to position its product— by advertising in a senior publication, by the apparent age of the model and with the phrase, "whatever her age."

"The Shape-Up That Works to Lift Years Off Your Eyes." (Illustration: Female model.)

Tonicite Firming Care is for "eyes that are ready for an extra measure of attention." It treats "all four signs of aging around the eyes." The beauty care industry is wooing mature women and looking forward to huge numbers of female baby boomers who are developing eye wrinkles as you read these words.

"Don't tarnish your silver."

An attractive silver-haired woman illustrates the benefits of the product in this effective ad for Jhirmack Hair Spray, "Specially formulated for silver, gray or graying hair."

(The media has taken to calling First Lady Barbara Bush, "The Silver Fox." She lives up to the billing.)

"Turn Time Into A Beautiful Advanatge." (Illustration: Female model.)

Billions of dollars are spent each year for beauty care and Lancome, Paris, is staking a claim for some of it with its new product, Forte-Vital, a skin firming serum. The product is one of many such beauty care products designed to reverse the signs of aging and "restore a firmer, more toned appearance to face and neck."

Miscellaneous

"We weren't born yesterday either. We're over fads and foolishiness and we've been waiting for a woman just like you. You can meet us on the pages of the Brownstone Studio Fashion Collection where fashion comes of age. Beautifully."

Brownstone Studio is one of many catalogs offering apparel designed for older women. Either women are not finding the sizes and styles they are looking for in the retail stores or they prefer mail order shopping. In any case, the success of catalogs catering to mature needs and preferences, tells us something about the pent-up demand for products designed for an aging America.

"Looks Like a Pump, Feels Like a Sneaker."

Easy Spirit Dress Shoes are responding to the older woman's search for good looks *and* comfort. Their ad says "you can walk for miles—and your feet won't feel a thing." It's a claim that women of all ages would respond to but the fact that this ad appeared in a senior magazine indicates where they think their real market is.

"'Jockey For Her is the best fitting underwear I've ever worn. It's so comfortable. And now my granddaughters wear Jockey for Girls'." (Illustration: Woman in underwear on phone, an inset shows same woman reading to granddaughters.)

The woman in the photograph is identified by name and the fact that she is a grandmother/Banker in Sheboygan, Wisconsin. Here is a real challenge: A product with a macho name, originally designed for men. The image has to be changed from male to female—and to an older female, at that. The ad succeeds because it is sexy without being vulgar and shows a real woman in life situations.

"Look Who's Reading Large Print Best Sellers." (Illustration: Middle age couple in an outdoor setting.)

The Doubleday Large Print Books ad removes the stigma of age from the need for large type. By implication it says, "Look, large print books aren't just for old people. A lot of younger people with poor vision enjoy them too." Consequently, seniors can order large print books without being reminded of their age and the reduced vision that comes with it. Besides, it lists some very good books at an attractive price.

"Putting New Meaning Into a Life-Long Relationship . . ."

In addition to a large phot of the Aluma-Lite motorhome being advertised, Holiday Rambler Corporation's ad shows mature hands holding each other fondly. The copy starts: "What could be better than the years you've already enjoyed? The years you have yet to experience." and ends with "Test drive one today and begin another life-long commitment . . . together."

"Life Is Only As Meaningful As You Make It."

New York University offers courses on a variety of subjects of interest to older adults. Their full-page advertisement in *The Best Years* highlights courses on new careers ("Over 55? What's Next?"), retirement planning, starting and managing your own business as well as courses which combine culture and travel. Right next to their sign-off logo is the slogan, "Why Shouldn't Learning Go On For A Lifetime?"

Index

About the Author

ROBERT MENCHIN, the author of *The Mature Market* is a recognized authority on the marketing of financial services and selling to seniors. A former Vice President of the Chicago Board of Trade, he is currently President of Chicago-based Mature Market Consultants.